♻ NatWest

BUSINESS
HANDBOOKS

*Small Books
with Big
Information*

health
and
safety

Third Edition

Alison Broadhurst

DERBY college
LEARNING RESOURCE
CENTRE

PITMAN
PUBLISHING

PITMAN PUBLISHING
128 Long Acre, London WC2E 9AN
Tel: +44(0)171 447 2000
Fax: +44(0)171 240 5771

A Division of Pearson Professional Limited

First published in Great Britain 1995
2nd edition 1995
3rd edition 1996

British Library Cataloguing in Publication Data
A CIP catalogue record for this book can be obtained from the British Library.

ISBN 0 273 62627 2

10 9 8 7 6 5 4 3 2 1

---

*The information in this book is intended as a general guide based upon the
legislation at the time of going to press. Neither the Bank, its staff nor the
author can accept liability for any loss arising as a result of reliance upon any
information contained herein and readers are strongly advised to obtain
professional advice on an individual basis.*

Typeset by Avocet Typeset, Brill, Aylesbury, Bucks
Printed and bound by Antony Rowe Ltd, Eastbourne

The Publishers' policy is to use paper manufactured from sustainable forests.

contents

preface to the third edition

The unstoppable Euro tide sweeps in and deposits Health and Safety Directives upon our shores before retreating to obtain fresh supplies. These Directives have to be expressed in the national legislation in the Member States of the European Union. John Masefield, writing in a completely different context and unaware of what lay ahead, said: '... for the running tide is a wild call and a clear call that cannot be denied'.

The Directives lead to legislation which makes new demands upon business and professional firms, large and small, and which extends existing law where gaps have been identified. Much depends upon the manner in which Euro-inspired legislation is enforced in the Member States. In the United Kingdom we must expect an insistence upon compliance but, it is hoped, with an admixture of commonsense by officials.

Conscientious officials draft the Regulations for this country while other officials draft the Approved Codes of Practice which explain the Regulations. Yet others draft guidance to explain the Codes of Practice and at the bottom of the pile – some would say the top – are those who design the colourful leaflets which highlight the essentials.

The Health and Safety Commission is currently seeking the views of small firms about health and safety requirements and their enforcement, with a view to lessening the burden. Deregulation is in hand and outdated laws are being rescinded, but this has made only a limited change so far because the 1974 Act and its regulations generally cover the same ground. Curiously, of the laws which have disappeared are those relating to the old type of outworker, and it may be conjectured that new laws will appear one day as more employees work at computers on company business at home.

Preface

It is not always easy for small undertakings to find out what is expected of them, but it is hoped that this book, concentrated though it is, will be of assistance to employers and others who accept that health and safety is an important aspect of life today.

Alison Broadhurst
April 1996

1

why bother?

Introduction

Modern health and safety legislation has its origins in a bill introduced in Parliament by Sir Robert Peel in 1802.

Since then the development of industry and then the massive flowering of technology have led to a greater need for health and safety control. Providing safe[1] conditions is no longer a matter of commonsense, if ever it was. There are technicalities involved in apparently mundane risks which today may be invisible and not detectable by the senses (e.g. various forms of radiation).

The development of this legislation, under the influence of the European Union, will cause the older law to become more patchier than ever as more bits are replaced by the new – but not always better – law. The long-established and succinct requirement for the 'secure fencing' of dangerous parts of machinery under the Factories Acts, which has proved valuable for some 60 years, has been replaced by more detailed demands under Regulations for Work Equipment. It has been said, with some justification, that the European-type legislation deals excessively with means rather than ends. But it is there and has to be obeyed.

An inherent part

Health and safety are twin threads running through every business or professional enterprise. A new enterprise is not born with a silver spoon in its mouth but a copy of the Health and Safety at Work Act. Even so, safety has to be integrated with the other aspects of running the business.

---

1 'Safety' generally includes health in this book.

There is a lot of other legislation, too. Some of it is relevant to a wide range of premises, being of general application – like the Fire Precautions Act 1971, for instance. Some of it only applies to factories, offices or shops or places of sport and various industrial activities. The Factories Act, in particular, has spawned a large family of regulations and the Health and Safety at Work Act emulates it by producing regulations and codes of practice. Some of these replace earlier sets of regulations, for example those relating to electricity, but others, like the ones for classification, packaging and labelling of dangerous substances, venture into new territory. More are to come. Some are affected by the European Directives which seek harmonisation among member countries.

This may all seem daunting but fortunately an individual firm will only be subject to those regulations which are specific to its activities. The regulations governing electricity will in practice be of universal application but those relating to lead or highly flammable liquids, for instance, will only be applicable where such materials are used or stored. The 1974 Act, as already stated, applies to all.

Criminal safety law

The Factories Act, the Health and Safety at Work Act and the others of this type, together with their regulations, are part of the criminal law. The legislation lays down the standards and the areas of their application. You have to carry out what Parliament has decided and if you fail, you are liable to be punished under the law. This usually means a fine but can lead to imprisonment in extreme cases.

Inspectors of the central government body, the Health and Safety Executive (HSE), and of local government (usually the Environmental Health Officers) enforce this law. Many, but not all, small firms (e.g. shops) will be inspected by the latter body. Their powers are outlined in Chapter 18 as are those of the HSE.

HSE Inspectors had advised the management of a factory producing magnetrons that the existing screen round a test area was inadequate and should be replaced by a fully interlocked enclosure. But this advice was not taken. One day an operator, seeing a magnetron jammed in the test area reached round the screen to remedy matters but was electrocuted on accidentally touching a 4000 volt AC live contact, earthing it through being also in contact with the metal of the conveyor. The employers were prosecuted and fined £2,000 plus costs.

Common law

This, 'the basic law of the land', deals with the rights of persons who have been injured as a result of your negligence. Most claims under this heading are made by employees or ex-employees. However, the number of customers who make claims if, for instance, they fall while on your premises and are injured, is increasing.

Members of the public may also claim if they have been injured, because of what they believe to be your negligence, even if the accident occurred when not on your premises. This can happen, for instance, if you use a crane with the jib overhanging the street and it drops its load on a hapless pedestrian passing by.

A child aged two-and-a half was visiting a factory Open Day with his parents but managed to wander unnoticed towards the edge of a landing where there was a hand rail. He climbed under this and fell through a gap. The company was advised to provide additional barriers to keep visitors on designated routes.

You are liable in law for what your employees do in the course of their employment. If one is careless and causes injury to another employee – or anyone else – you will generally be liable. Today every employer must be insured under the employer's liability law to cover claims which may be made against a firm by an injured employee. In practice, you may deem it wise to take additional cover for other accidents, too. Failure to insure for employer's liability attracts a very heavy financial penalty but you cannot insure against being prosecuted – this may happen for any breach of the criminal safety law.

Claims based on your alleged negligence, whether by an employee or anyone else, are part of the civil law.

3

How to get advice

To find out what the requirements are, you need advice. One important source is the inspector, whether of HSE or local government. Inspectors are required to advise as well as enforce.

There are other sources of advice, e.g. from employers' associations, technical and trade journals and private consultants. Commercial firms engaged in safety-related products also offer advice within their own fields. For instance, if you need protective wear, reputable manufacturers can advise about the suitability of different products for the particular use you have in mind.

Because of the many technicalities, apart from legislation, there is a large and increasing array of official publications to help you. These range from detailed booklets to leaflets and pocket notes designed for workpeople. Many are issued free by HSE and may be obtained as a result of a telephone call.

Such official publications are generally practical, and manage to avoid legal jargon in advising you what you should do. Last but, it is hoped, not least, this book seeks to advise and guide you as far as space permits.

The scope of the subject

The scope of the subject is wide but you need to identify which parts apply to your business. This will depend on what you do and how you do it. Small firms have a significant accident rate and suffer most if a key person is absent.

One small ceramics firm faced liquidation when unexpectedly high lead blood levels were found in their employees. Only the advice of the HSE and the firm's own cooperation saved their business.

All firms must have a safe system of work, including a safe place of work, safe machinery, plant and equipment, and safety in the use of dangerous substances, handling, storage and methods of work, as well as proper instruction, training and supervision – and management. All these subjects and the way they are used and how they are integrated into a whole system are included within the meaning of the term 'system of work'. Many accidents occur because the system is defective.

The place of work

The term 'place of work' is used in at least two senses. It refers to the whole place itself, such as an office block, a school or a farm. It also refers, perhaps more often, to the actual workplace of individuals and the immediate environment. Thus it refers to the display screen equipment (VDU) used by an employee, the seating, lighting and other features of the working environment there. A lot of the requirements for health and safety at work are concentrated on the place of work in this sense.

Buildings as a whole and individual workshops, offices and other places have to be structurally sound and provided with adequate means of escape in case of fire. Inspectors have power to close down unsafe places without warning.

The working environment is important. Suitable heating, ventilation, lighting and freedom from harmful dusts, fumes, gases and excessive noise have to be ensured. Even outdoor sites may present hazards such as overhead high voltage power lines which may be accidentally contacted by, say, tipper lorries and cranes. If your employees have to work in the premises of others (including domestic premises), you still have a duty to protect them. For example, one firm's drivers had complained about unsafe means of access at bakeries where they delivered sacks of flour. To deal with the matter, the employers sent someone to check these and make suitable arrangements with the bakery firms.

Machinery, plant and equipment

All dangerous parts of all machinery must be securely guarded. In many cases there are known standards, some of which are set out in regulations. Lifting plant such as cranes have an unnerving habit of falling over from time to time or dropping a load. All such plant and equipment have to be safely designed, constructed used and maintained, and periodically examined by a competent person, usually an insurance company surveyor. His reports have to be kept available for inspection.

A safe electrical installation is essential for electricity is a killer. No unqualified person should be allowed to tamper with it. New machinery should comply with statutory standards but sometimes a machine slips through the net. Watch out for this. You will need to check second-hand equipment particularly carefully because it is your responsibility once you use any plant or machinery. Hired plant also needs to be checked by you. Beware of home-made contrivances. Improvisation is a fruitful source of danger.

In a furniture-restoring business a curious artefact was devised to flash off solvents from french polish. This was fashioned from a piece of timber and an unguarded electrical element. After one look, the inspector issued a Prohibition ('stop') Notice.

Dangerous substances

There is increasing concern with ill-health at work. During 1995, the HSE launched a major campaign to reduce ill-health associated with work. It pointed out that 2.2 million people annually suffer ill-health caused or exacerbated by work. The campaign is supported, among others, by one of the world's leading asthma specialists and it is planned to run for at least three years. The range of health concerns, from strains to asthma, will be discussed with employers with the object of alerting them to the seriousness of the situation – and, of course, advising them on suitable action to take. It may be noted that improvements in health are not necessarily either difficult or expensive and they benefit everybody. Individuals gain by having better health and the employer has the bonus of less sickness absence as well as a healthier work force.

Review all substances which you use or store and check on their more unsavoury characteristics. Always use the safest material for any job. But if you do have to use dangerous substances, find out what precautions have to be taken. There are, for instance, flammables in various forms, solids, fumes, gases, dusts. Even loose paper lying on the floor in the packing department can burn nicely, given a sporting chance. Find out also about any regulations applying to the materials you have.

In one case liquefied petroleum (LP) gas escaped from a fuel tank believed to be empty. But as two employees walked out of the small factory the gas-air mixture exploded, demolishing the building, their jobs and probably the small firm itself.

Many materials are potentially dangerous to health when breathed (e.g. asbestos or lead), or when in contact with the skin (e.g. some solvents), and even a simple material like flour can cause dermatitis.

Handling and storage

We seem to be becoming a nation of bad backs. Not only do we undertake an excessive amount of manual handling but we do not train people enough in safe means of doing it. It is in the interests of productivity as well as safety that manhandling of goods should be minimised. Accidents happen not only from lifting excessive weights but particularly as a result of unsafe methods. This is discussed further in Chapter 10 on manual handling.

A common fault is to underestimate the amount of space needed for handling and storage. This should be sufficient for dealing with raw materials and bought-in parts and components, work in progress, finished goods awaiting despatch or in temporary storage and those sudden deliveries which take up so much space. Some substances like petroleum can only be stored if you have the requisite licence. In some cases regulations may lay down the conditions under which you store materials such as LP gas. Waste products come in many guises and you will need to foresee what kind and amount of waste you will produce. Proper arrangements must be made for their disposal in accordance with current legislation. Some, like asbestos, must be disposed of only by approved means.

Adopting a policy

You are in control of the work and decide how it will be carried out. The methods you lay down need to be checked from time to time to ensure that your instructions are followed. Unsafe practices invite trouble.

In one small works leak testing of cylinders was done in an unsafe manner which also tended to deform the tanks being tested. An inspector, considering the method dangerous ordered the firm to introduce a safer method. To the firm's delight this also improved their productivity.

A positive policy is needed. All but the tiniest of firms have to produce a written safety policy statement. Many matters require your decision from the start – for example, will employees be allowed to smoke at work? Sometimes it is prohibited by law, e.g. if there is an unusual fire risk or where poisonous substances are used. Or, do you intend to employ young persons under 18? If so are you prepared to give them the extra attention that they need?

Training

Training of all levels of personnel at work in health and safety at work, whether they are employed or self-employed – and including employers – is a basic necessity. It may take place off the job or on the job, or both. Managers can usefully attend seminars set up by employers' associations and other bodies. They need the know-how as they have responsibilities which they cannot properly carry out unless they are well informed. There are apprenticeships available and courses of all kinds at local technical colleges for employees. The Construction Industry Training Board for instance has a long history of promoting training which is highly regarded.

One problem encountered by employees on returning from external training is that the conditions back on their ordinary jobs do not always permit them to apply what they have learnt. This should not happen if their superiors also have the necessary knowledge. It is not acceptable to regard experience as a substitute, although this is often sometimes misunderstood.

A 60-year old man of nearly a lifetime's experience of operating woodworking machinery could have been killed when some wood flew out of his machine – and this had happened once before. It was outside his experience and knowledge that this was extremely dangerous and he did not even report the first incident. He had to report the second one because he was injured. To make matters worse, his supervisor was not trained either, in spite of Regulations demanding that both should have received adequate training.

New National Vocational Qualifications (NVQs) in England and Wales and Scottish Vocational Qualifications (SVQs) have been introduced and are being further developed to meet the demand for work-based qualifications. They are available freely, without prior qualifications, and at five levels. The City and Guilds of London Institute is the awarding body for NVQs and The Scottish Vocational Educational Council for SVQs.

One firm allowed two young male employees to work alone at dangerous woodworking machines contrary to regulations without adequate supervision or training. The inevitable happened and one was injured. He no doubt carries the scars to this day.

All employees in fact need training and instruction and to be informed about the hazards and precautions of their work. But young persons have to receive extra care in training.

Planning and budgeting

Planning for safety starts at Day One and continues for ever. This has to be reviewed from time to time and certainly when changes are made, for instance, on the installation of new plant. Some cost will be incurred if only for the keeping of records . All costs obviously need to be budgeted for from the beginning. But not all safety matters are costly – some even save money (e.g. by requiring new methods).

In planning, bear in mind that safety is more than just accident prevention. That term means what it says, the prevention of accidents. But if they do occur you need to have some plans for dealing with them. This is the 'damage limitation' stage. Thus you control flammables and sources of ignition to prevent fire breaking out. But if it does break out you then need fire fighting and other precautions. Both

9

aspects have to figure in your planning – and not just for fire of course. Today all persons have to be protected from danger arising from your activities wherever they are carried out. Employees, customers and other visitors, members of the general public (including trespassers) and the self-employed are under the protection of safety legislation now.

2

factories, offices, shops and farms

The importance of factory legislation • What is a factory? •
Offices and shops • Basic standards • Farms

The importance of factory legislation

Factory legislation from its beginnings in the early nine-
teenth century has matured alongside the many industrial
and technological changes. In the course of this development
there have been an ever-increasing amount of Case Law. For
over 30 years it centred on the Factories Act 1961 and its
host of Regulations, Orders, etc. Now this Act, although still
alive and kicking, is slowly becoming riddled with gaps as
new legislation under the Health and Safety Act replaces it
piecemeal. A point which should be noted is that all new
requirements will either raise standards or maintain existing
ones where appropriate.

What is a factory?

The term 'factory' has a wider meaning than that of the
dictionary. It obviously includes premises where articles are
made. Also, by definition, it includes premises, even in the
open air, carried on as a business, where at least one person
is employed and in which: articles are altered (e.g. the
alterations workroom of a dress shop); articles are repaired
(e.g. a vehicle repair garage); articles are cleaned (e.g. a dry
cleaning works); articles are broken up (e.g. a scrap metal
works); articles are sorted incidentally to work in any
factory (e.g. sorting waste paper for use at a factory elsewhere); articles are adapted for sale (e.g. ripening bananas
by artificial heat).

Also included are such places as: abattoirs; a yard or dry dock
where ships or vessels are constructed, repaired or refitted;

premises where articles such as bottles or containers are washed or filled, or articles are packed incidentally to the purposes of any factory; laundries ancillary to another business (e.g. a hotel); printing works. Certain premises such as farms, mines and parts of quarries are excluded, being covered by other statutes e.g. the Health and Safety at Work Act.

Notional factories

In addition, some premises are expressly included as 'notional' factories. For instance these include: electrical stations (e.g. for the purpose of an industrial or commercial undertaking); some charitable and reformatory institutions where articles are made or adapted for sale; docks, wharfs and quays (including certain warehouses there); harbours or wet docks where constructing, repairing, refitting and breaking up a ship (as defined in merchant shipping legislation) are carried on; certain other work on ships in harbour or wet dock (e.g. cleaning out oil/fuel tanks or bilges); building operations (see Chapter 4); works of engineering construction (see Chapter 4).

Comprehensive though it is, this list of premises subject to the Factories Act is not complete but it indicates the more common kinds of small businesses. A factory may be any size, even a single room or part of one. You should make enquiries if you are in any doubt as you have to notify the inspector in writing before opening a factory.

Offices and shops

The Offices, Shops and Railway Premises Act 1963 is modelled on the Factories Act but has a lesser technical content. An office is a building (or part) where administration, writing, book-keeping, sorting papers, filing, typing, duplicating, machine calculating, drawing, the editorial preparation of matter for publication, handling money, telephone and telegraph operating is carried on and someone is employed. As in the factory legislation, the purpose is to protect the employees. All offices and shops are also subject to the Health and Safety at Work Act. A 'shop' has its ordinary meaning and extends to other places used for retail trade or business, and to wholesale warehouses (except docks warehouses listed as factories – see above). 'Retail trade or business' includes catering establishments open to the public, retail auction sales and libraries for lending books and periodicals for gain.

Basic standards

In so far as similar plant and equipment is used, the safety standards for factories and offices are similar. Examples are those relating to lifts and hoists, pallet trucks and belt conveyors. Environmental standards are similar too (e.g. for cleanliness, heating and ventilation).

Farms

Agriculture is another area of activity which has had its special legislation. This has developed since the 1950s and today some, but not all, of this specific legislation remains in force. For instance, there have been Regulations for power take-offs and for threshers and balers. The former have been revoked but the latter have been modified only.

But some machinery is used in industry as well as farms (e.g. circular saws which were regulated in agriculture in 1959) but had already been subject to Regulations in industry since 1922. Some rationalisation seems to be called for but, at the time of writing, the agriculture regulations have been modified and the industrial ones re-written. The Work Equipment Regulations, verbose though they are, have caused these changes.

It is rumoured that some farmers are somewhat bemused by all this.

3

moving to new premises?

Is there enough space? • Stairways • Lifts and hoists • Floors • Doors and gates • Windows • Fire precautions • Heating and ventilation • Washing and toilet facilities • The general rule

Is there enough space?

In addition to checking for general soundness in premises which you intend to occupy, there are some pitfalls to avoid. You may be satisfied that there is adequate room for your plant, furniture and employees, but what about the things you have to store? Is there sufficient space, especially after a new delivery? If you use flammable liquids, is there a suitable safe store? If your business prospers, you may need more space for people and goods perhaps – is there room for expansion? What about vehicles delivering goods to you – is there a yard? If not, how will you handle them? If there is a yard, is there turning room for vehicles? If not, you may need to supply an assistant to help drivers to back out – blind reversing causes many accidents. You will no doubt check car parking facilities too.

There should be adequate space for people to reach their workplaces safely and to move about. Floor obstructions such as computer cables should not be allowed in passageways. There should be adequate height in workrooms, but if in old buildings there are old beams which cannot be moved, warning signs should be marked clearly on them.

The volume of the room (i.e. height x length x width) should allow at least 11 cubic metres per person. But heights above 3m have to be ignored in this calculation. In certain special structures such as retail kiosks or machine control cabs, this standard does not apply.

Stairways

Are the stairways in good condition, fitted with handrails and well lighted? Check the light switches for staircase lights. Do employees have to grope up or down in the dark until reaching a switch? Make sure that no doors open directly on to stairs. Remember that you and your staff are likely to have to carry things up or down at times. Spiral staircases are often unsuitable.

Lifts and hoists

Perhaps there is a lift for passengers and goods. If so, confirm that the landlord has it properly examined and maintained, if the premises are shared with others. Otherwise you may be responsible. Is there a hoist for goods? And if so, is it suitable for the things you handle? Regular examination and maintenance are essential.

A small firm had a laboratory located on the top floor of a three-storey building. They overlooked the need for a lift and employees had to carry full gas cylinders up. On occasion, one man would do this alone and he was found dragging a cylinder upstairs and banging it on every step as he did so. This was dangerous.

Floors

Floors should be free of defects such as holes, unevenness and slipperiness and slopes should not be excessively steep. If used by disabled people, slopes and ramps often need a handrail. If your processes may cause spillage, pay particular attention to drainage.

Traffic routes for vehicles should be planned so that people are not exposed to danger, the area round doorways being especially liable to lead to accidents.

If you have plant of any kind which imposes a heavy load on the floor, check the safe floor loading of any upper floor where you propose to install it. A fork-lift truck, for instance, is for ground floor and outdoor use as it imposes too heavy a concentrated load for an upper floor. Even in new workshops, problems may arise.

15

A new annexe attached to a factory building had cable ducts made in the floor which had been covered over with concrete slabs about 300 mm (12 in) square and 25 mm (1 in) thick. They had no steel reinforcement, having been installed for light workshop traffic. When machinery was being installed, a portable gantry mounted on four wheels was used to move some of the machine parts. Whilst in use, some of the concrete cover slabs fractured under one of its wheels. This caused the gantry to tilt and trap one of the men pushing it. Calculations revealed that the load on this wheel was nearly half a ton which was too heavy a concentrated load for the floor.

Doors and gates

These need to be of suitable construction (e.g. sliding doors should be fitted with devices to prevent the doors coming off their tracks when in use). Any door which may be opened from either side should be so designed that, when closed, there is a clear view of the other side, both ways.

Windows

Windows and walls and other transparent surfaces at or below waist level should be made of safety materials or be adequately protected against accidental breakage. There is an exception for glasshouses.

Windows and skylights should be capable of being opened and closed without danger and if there is a danger of anyone falling from a height there should be devices limiting the amount of opening. They should be such that they can be cleaned safely (e.g. from inside) or there should be suitably placed anchorages for safety harnesses to be worn by window cleaners.

Fire precautions

Fire precautions are obviously of extreme importance and you will need to clarify who is responsible for what, if you share a building. Some, at least, of the responsibility rests on you. Means of detecting fire, sounding the alarm, fire fighting and means of escape for everyone in the building need attention. A Certificate of Means of Escape in Case of Fire is needed. (See Chapter 7.)

Heating and ventilation

Heating and ventilation are central to health and comfort in the working environment. If you are going to use the top floor of a building for sedentary work, there may be problems of low temperature, at least on cold Monday mornings, after being unheated over the weekend. If you share a building, check how much control you have over the heating system. Check also, where appropriate, the arrangements to prevent Legionnaire's disease.

Washing and toilet facilities

Washing and toilet facilities are often shared where there are two or more tenants. Check that there is sufficient provision for everyone and ascertain whether the landlord accepts responsibility for cleaning and maintenance.

The general rule

The general rule in shared occupancy of buildings is that the landlord deals with those parts of the premises used by two or more tenants whilst the individual firm is responsible for its own part. The contract should be checked on the matter before you sign.

4

construction sites and other workplaces

Construction work • Main causes of accidents • Accident prevention • Site planning • Construction management • Other workplaces

Construction work

This has a distressing safety record in which small firms, sadly, play a prominent part. Construction work includes building operations and works of engineering construction. Concerned about the record of small construction sites, the HSE has again stressed that health and safety is an integral part of the setting out of work from the start. The CDM (Construction, Design and Management) Regulations have taken up this point,

Building operations

The term 'building operation' includes not only the construction of buildings but also their structural alteration, repair, maintenance (including repainting, redecoration and external cleaning of a structure), demolition and preparation for and laying of the foundation.

Works of engineering construction

The term 'works of engineering construction' includes: the construction of any railway line or siding except one upon an existing railway; the construction, structural alteration, repair or demolition of any dock, harbour, inland navigation, tunnel, bridge, viaduct, waterworks, reservoir, pipeline, aqueduct, sewer, sewage works, gasholder, steel or reinforced concrete structure (other than a building), road, airfield, sea defence works, river works, other similar civil engineering works, pipeline for conveyance of anything except water. There are some exceptions with regard to work upon a railway or tramway.

Main causes of accidents

Fatalities and serious injuries arise especially because of people falling from a height (e.g. scaffolding); being struck by a moving vehicle; being trapped by something collapsing or overturning (e.g. a dumper); being struck by various other moving objects (e.g. falling loads).

Serious injuries are also regularly recorded as being caused by handling, lifting and carrying things; slips, trips and falls on the same level; striking against something; contact with machinery or material being operated on by machine (e.g. concrete mixers); exposure to or contact with harmful substances. Electricity causes many accidents both directly by electric shock and indirectly when contact with live conductors on a site leads to a person falling from a height. All aspects of electrical safety should be considered at the design and planning stage as well as during actual construction work.

Work is proceeding on the consolidation of the existing and ageing Construction Regulations for safety, currently spread over three main sets. Existing requirements will be retained and new ones introduced.

Accident prevention

Falling people characterise the industry as they tumble off roofs, scaffolding, ladders and other places. A clue to safeguarding is the figure of 2 metres (6 ft 6 in). Whenever there is a risk of falling this distance, the fullest precautions are needed although lesser falls also cause injuries.

Children

Unfortunately, sites often attract children who see them as an interesting playing area. While parents have a responsibility to warn children to keep off them, those who manage construction sites also have a duty to do all they can to exclude children. For instance, sites should be enclosed and locked as far as possible; materials should be securely locked up and plant rendered safe against interference. Sites are a lure to children.

Several schoolboys were larking about on a site after working hours when one of them found a drum containing a substance which, not surprisingly, he did not identify. He then found an old glove, filled it with this material and threw it at one of the others in fun. But the material was caustic soda which had been left accessible. The schoolboy who was struck by the glove sustained nasty burns to his head and hands.

Roof work

Roof work produces a regular quota of accidents often involving serious injuries. Workpeople fall off the edges of roofs and through fragile ones like asbestos roofs.

A partner in a firm of general builders fell 3.4 m (11 ft) through the asbestos cement roof of a factory. He was carrying out minor repairs working on his own, before falling to his death. A single plank 228 mm (9 in) wide was found at the approaches to the roof.

Before requiring anyone to work on a roof consider whether the work could be done in another, safer way. Could the job be carried out from underneath, standing on a platform, for example? There are strict regulations requiring the use of crawling boards or ladders with barriers to prevent anyone falling off the edge. Other precautions may be needed too, dependent on the circumstances.

Scaffolding

There are various types of scaffolding but all have to be well constructed, stable and suitably secured against collapse. Only experienced persons should be allowed to erect scaffolds and there are specialist firms available. The walkways should be kept clear of obstructions and free from slippery surfaces. Care is needed to prevent overloading. Guard rails and toe boards or equivalent guarding is needed and proper access has to be provided. Scaffolds should be inspected before being used for the first time, after any alteration or following severe weather. Regular examinations at weekly intervals by a competent person are also required and the results must be entered in a register kept for the purpose. This is Form 91, Part 1.

Tower scaffolds are often used by painters and others for lighter work requiring movement from place to place. They should be obtained from a reputable supplier, safe design and construction being important. There are restrictions on the height-to-base ratio so that the centre of gravity is not too high, causing instability. The working platform should be closely boarded with boards of adequate thickness. Guard rails and toe boards have to be provided on all sides of the working platform.

An electrician and his mate were installing trunking beneath a ceiling. They were using a mobile scaffold tower made from lightweight metal scaffolding. The working platform was about 3 m (10 ft) above ground level and the tower itself was about 2.1 m (7 ft) long and about 0.9 m (3 ft) wide. Instead of climbing up on the inside of the short side, the electrician began to climb up outside the long side, using the cross members as a foothold. To make matters worse, his mate did not wait but began to climb up at the same time, following the electrician. This was enough to cause the scaffold to overturn so that both men were injured.

Ladders

Every ladder and folding stepladder must be of good construction, of suitable and sound material and of adequate strength for the purpose for which it is used. Its proper maintenance is important. Timber ladders must never be painted – this hides defects.

For safety purposes, ladders are divided into three classes. **Class 1** is suitable for construction work where the ladder is in frequent use and subject to substantial loads. **Class 2** is intended for lighter trades such as decorating, where relatively low loads are involved. **Class 3** is for light use (e.g. domestic purposes).

A self-employed roofing contractor carrying a batch of roofing tiles fell to his death from about 4.5 m (15 ft) off a two-stage timber extension ladder fitted with aluminium rungs. The

21

ladder, which was some three years old, failed when both stiles snapped near the base of the upper section. The HSE investigated the accident and said that the ladder may have been overloaded. A Class 1 ladder should have been used instead of the Class 2 one which the roofer had employed.

In use, ladders should be erected on a firm, level base and anti-slip sleeves may be needed. The head of the ladder should rest on a firm, solid surface. The '1 in 4' rule should be observed, that is the slope should be such that the foot of the ladder is one metre out for every four metres of height. Ladders should be securely lashed near the top against displacement, or other adequate means should be used where top lashing is not possible. Having a second person to 'foot' the ladder is only effective for short ladders.

Do not use metal ladders or timber ladders with metal reinforcement where there is a risk of electrical contact (with live conductors). All ladders should extend at least 1.05 m (3 ft 6 in) above the place of landing. All ladders should be regularly inspected for such defects as splits, warping, worn or missing rungs, damaged feet and the like. Defective ladders should be taken out of use for repair or scrapped. They should not be consigned to a pile of rubbish for disposal but removed entirely, otherwise someone may come along and pick them up and use them.

Excavations

Accidents caused by the collapse of excavations are usually serious and sometimes fatal. They are often caused by inadequate support. Other matters to avoid are placing materials and moving plant too close to the edge. The sides of large, open excavations should be battered where appropriate. All should be inspected daily and thoroughly examined every seven days. A record of these examinations should be kept in the official register (Form 91, Part 1, Section B).

Weather

A subject of importance to all who work outside is the weather. Bad weather can convert a safe site into a dangerous one in minutes. Walkways can suddenly become treacherously slippery, the sides of untimbered trenches can be loosened dangerously and this could lead to collapse. High winds wreak their own kind of havoc, blowing things over, and can present a nasty hazard to anyone carrying a large sheet of material.

Demolition

You need a properly experienced person to supervise demolition work.

As a preliminary, attention has to be paid to any risks in connection with services such as water, gas and electricity. Risks of flooding, explosive accumulations of gas, electrocution or striking underground cables have all to be taken seriously. Every necessary precaution against unplanned collapse must obviously be taken.

A number of two-storey cottages, which were 70 years old, were being demolished. They formed a terrace of five, but three of them had already been partly demolished. This earlier work had left a 110 mm (4.5 in) wall which was 6.4 m (21 ft) long and 7.3 m (24 ft) high, standing. At the extreme ends of the wall were two short portions of 230 mm (9 in) brickwork – the remains of the front and rear walls. The contractor planned to weaken the wall so that the workmen could push it over manually. This never happened because the wall collapsed whilst being weakened and a workman was killed. The accident could have been prevented if the wall had been shored against collapse and demolition carried on piecemeal. The person in charge had failed to appreciate how dangerous the wall was.

Site planning

Preliminary work includes notifying the HSE within seven days on Form 10 that construction work is starting (unless it is expected to be completed in less than six weeks) and any necessary contact with competent bodies (e.g. with the electricity authority to locate existing services and, where necessary, to isolate overhead supplies).

Ensure that statutory forms such as registers are available.

Plan the health and welfare facilities whether shared with others or not. These include suitable arrangements for taking meals, drinking water, washing and toilet facilities, clothing, accommodation and first aid. Check whether there is a telephone available in case of emergency. If no telephone is available, ensure that transport is always available in case of emergency.

If you intend to use highly flammable materials (e.g. LP gas), make proper arrangements for storage and use. Where special fire precautions are needed, as when working in or on a large building, check these beforehand and inform your employees.

On one small building site there was a small mess hut provided with a gas ring and a gas oven, each with its own cylinder of LP gas. The kettle was heating merrily on the gas ring but as meal time approached it was found necessary to replace the gas cylinder for the oven. One man therefore fetched a full cylinder whilst another man removed the almost empty one. Unfortunately, this man turned the control 'on' instead of 'off'. Mercifully, no one was seriously hurt but the resulting explosion destroyed the hut.

Construction management

A new approach is now necessary in managing construction projects, in the interests of health and safety. In particular, new duties have been placed on clients, clients' agents (where appointed), designers and contractors.

The long-term result should be better safety for those engaged on the construction work and for those who have later to use and maintain the buildings and other structures.

Co-ordination of the safety aspects is needed and overall responsibility at the design and planning stages is put upon an appointed planning supervisor who must also be responsible for ensuring that a health and safety plan is prepared. There must be a file to record health and safety information – this has been likened to a maintenance manual.

These new regulations (in force from 31 March 1995) require those concerned to become familiar with the details which are too many to record here. (See Chapter 15.)

Other workplaces

All places have their particular health and safety problems as well as commoner ones. A few examples of some of the special features for a number of different kinds of workplaces illustrate this.

Catering establishments

The number of accidents reported in these premises has been rising remorselessly for some years and, to make matters worse, there is good reason to believe that not all reportable accidents are in fact notified to the Local Authority (or HSE where appropriate).

Slips, trips and falls are the main causes of accidents in the hotel and catering industry generally. Simple things like water, grease or bits of vegetables spilled on to the floor present a hazard, and arrangements should be made on a permanent basis for spillages to be cleaned up without delay.

Kitchen equipment can be quite dangerous mechanically and some machines (e.g. vegetable slicing machines and power-operated meat mincers) are designated as specially dangerous. There is a risk of fire from oil, especially when being heated. Grease which collects in ventilation ducts will tend to spread any fire which occurs.

Sports and leisure centres

Among the safety problems are those relating to the fact that members of the public as well as staff will be on the premises. Ensure that access to gymnasium equipment is available only to adults and that adequate supervision is provided. For wet places like the surrounds of swimming pools and even the showers, take precautions against persons slipping. Have safe surfaces, beware of sudden changes of surfaces or hidden steps, and clean and drain the showers so that there is not a build-up of slippery material there.

Outdoor leisure activities have to be assessed for risk under current Regulations. Accidents in such places have recently received some media publicity.

A local authority was prosecuted by the HSE under the

Management Regulations. It was alleged that a proper risk assessment had not been carried out with reference to rock climbing there. It was also alleged that the local authority had failed to monitor preventive or protective measures. An instructor was personally prosecuted also.

Caravan parks

The road system should be planned for safety and if you have shower baths in a separate building, observe precautions to prevent people slipping. Also, arrange for an emergency alarm in the shower block to summon help in case of accident. First aid provision should take account of the number of people on the site.

Nursing homes

The risk of persons, particularly patients, falling out of windows is a real one and a number of fatalities are recorded each year. When carrying out the statutory risk assessment, attention to this point is very important. Modifications, where needed, must be carried out (e.g. by restricting the size of openings and by fitting safety glass).

Patients can be remarkably resourceful at squeezing through small spaces when determined and this needs to be borne in mind. Those in charge of such establishments must also remember that accidents – other than very minor ones – to staff, visitors or patients are notifiable.

The lifting and carrying of patients is demanding, so nurses and others who do this work need to be adequately trained. The amount of lifting and carrying should in any case be minimised, for example by the layout, so as to limit the distances involved. Wherever possible, mechanical lifting aids should be provided, ranging from individual personal slinging devices to lifts.

Educational establishments

Of all places, these should set an example and show students, pupils, lecturers, teachers and other employees that safety is not only taken seriously but that it is an integral part of running the establishment.

At one university there was a record of false fire alarms

26

which the authorities failed to remedy. The practice grew up therefore of ignoring them in spite of the building being a multi-story one. One professor, among other academics, was always to be found grinning at the window on an upper floor, looking down at the quadrangle where more cautious souls, who had vacated the building, were congregating.

But there is a rising tide of accidents in education generally. One in every 20 accidents reported to the HSE come from the education sector. Bearing in mind that the totality of accidents reported to the HSE includes industrial and other work places, this is as shocking a statistic as it may be a surprising one. Fatalities are included and in 1994, the last year for which statistics have, at the time of writing, been published, there were 12 fatalities, seven of them being to students or pupils and the rest to employees of various grades.

Urgent action is need in education to improve safety standards, including the following:

- update the statutory policy statement
- appoint specific persons to oversee safety
- ensure that these appointees are given the time and opportunity to be trained
- ensure that they have adequate support
- assess the main risks
- hold a complete inspection every term
- apply remedial action promptly
- produce an internal annual report on the matter

In some establishments there are laboratories with dangerous materials but in all there are likely to be chemicals for cleaning purposes. The manufacturer's recommendations should always be followed carefully. Cleaners should be provided with gloves and other protective wear as necessary and be made to wear them. In laboratories they will need to take special care with waste bins which may contain contaminated material and glassware. The safe disposal of all waste is a matter for the management to arrange.

School caretakers, for example, can be exposed to high concentrations of fumes when removing clinker and ash from solid fuel boilers. Advice should be sought from boiler manufacturers or solid fuel promotion bodies. Be aware of what is being stored and used, and ensure precautions are taken. The basic rule remains: use the safest material for any job and in the minimum amount. Chemicals should never be put into milk bottles or other unsuitable and unlabelled containers. It is a recipe for disaster to someone one day.

Farms

The dangers pertinent to farms and the safeguards required would need a whole book to outline. Here only a few points can be identified although what is said in all chapters is of relevance to farms. In agriculture, farmers, their employees, other farm workers and, sadly, children are exposed to various hazards. One unusual feature is that nearly a quarter of the accidents notified in agriculture occur to those over 65 years of age. Probably older men remain at work more than in other industries and, reliable and experienced though they generally are, they should not be expected to do the same lifting, etc. that they did when younger. They themselves need to realise that they may have slower reaction times and are likely to be somewhat less sprightly than in earlier years.

Tractors cause a number of accidents and, like road transport accidents, these tend to lead to serious injuries. It is hoped that agricultural college courses stress this matter. Some of the basic safety precautions which are often overlooked are:

- controls are misused
- hitching is not done correctly
- mounting not done safely
- dismounting not done safely
- machinery and moving parts are approached before fully stopped (i.e. at rest)
- workmen place themselves in positions where they are liable to be struck by the tractor or its attachments
- the tractor is operated on sloping ground

A general farm worker was intending to grease part of the bale grab of a front-end loader. Accordingly, he raised the loader, switched off the engine and placed himself between the loader and the front end of the tractor. But, unknown to him, the loader slowly descended and trapped his neck between the loader cross bar and the front of the tractor. He had failed to prop up the raised hydraulic equipment before going underneath it. Subsequent investigation indicated that the seals of the manual lift rams of the loader might have been worn so as to permit the downward creep of the loader.

'Agriculture' which here includes not only farming but also horticulture and forestry, is a major industry with its own special problems as well as those shared by other commercial undertakings. One special feature is the presence of children, although parents should prevent their offspring from trespassing into areas of risk. As there are dangerous machines and toxic substances like pesticides, special care is obviously necessary.

Safety is important on fish farms. The construction and maintenance of the installations, the provision of guard rails, foot rails, safe working surfaces, vehicle ways, and various means of rescue are among a number of essential safeguards. Diving regulations apply to diving operations both inside and outside cages. (These also apply to divers in other places of work.) Life jackets should be provided and worn at fish farms and at such places as oyster beds and areas where boats are hired out to the public either for fishing or for other recreational activities.

5

what facilities should be provided?

Washing facilities • Sanitary accommodation •
Eating facilities • Clothing accommodation • First aid •
Seating

Basic facilities for health and safety are required for all employees in every firm. The main ones are:

- washing facilities and sanitary accommodation
- eating facilities
- clothing accommodation
- first aid
- seating
- protective wear

They have to be provided by you.

Washing facilities

These should include wash-basins with warm and cold water laid on, soap and clean towels (or the equivalent). The basic standard is a minimum of one basin for five or fewer employees. Obviously for larger numbers, more wash stations are required (e.g. at least 3 for 26 to 50 employees and 5 for 76 to 100 employees). For places remote from sources of running water, containers of water will be needed, as well as soap etc. An adequate supply of drinking water is also required in all cases.

Where facilities are shared with other firms, for instance in office blocks, make sure that these minimum standards are met. When the washing facilities are part of a toilet area, these minimum numbers of basins must be met for men and women separately. Showers or baths are required in some cases (e.g.where substances handled are liable to contaminate the skin).

30

Sanitary accommodation

Separate provision must usually be made for men and women. The facilities should be partitioned off so as to secure privacy and there should be an intervening ventilated space between the accommodation and workroom.

Sanitary accommodation should be provided on a building site. At temporary sites and those without nearby sewers, suitable chemical closets are required.

Eating facilities

Where meals are regularly taken at the workplace and where lead or other substances liable to contaminate food are used, facilities for eating meals are needed. Precautions are essential to protect non-smokers from tobacco smoke (e.g. by segregating the areas for each group). Canteens are not normally needed for small premises, but some arrangements should be made for meal breaks. There should be suitable facilities for pregnant employees. Tea- and coffee-making machines about the premises may be provided. If LP gas cylinders are used for heating gas rings or ovens, take care to ensure that they are carefully handled. (See Chapter 7.)

Clothing accommodation

This is required under two headings:

- outdoor clothing
- protective clothing

Provision should be made for outdoor clothing during working hours. This must be secure, especially against theft, and means of drying should be provided. If you use a portable electric fire, care is needed to prevent fire and the appliance should not be placed too close to the clothing.

Accommodation for protective clothing – and items such as footwear, safety helmets and gloves also – is necessary. What has to be provided obviously depends on the nature of the item: for work with lead, for instance, adequate changing and storage facilities are needed.

First aid

Generally, only simple facilities are needed unless some special risk arises. In practice, if people other than your employees regularly come on to your premises, you should bear them in mind when deciding what to provide. This applies to customers in a shop or students in a school, for instance. The main points to consider are:

- the number of first aid boxes to be provided
- their location
- their contents
- qualified first-aiders
- outside help available

You have to make adequate and suitable provision for your particular circumstances. You therefore need to review your premises and activities to assess what your needs are. What you provide should be tailor-made by you for your firm.

For most small compact establishments a single box may be enough but more may be needed if your employees are dispersed over a wide area. A box should be readily accessible to everyone, so it should be suitably located. If your employees work alone or in isolated locations (e.g. on farms), you should provide small travelling kits. If your employees work on a building site together with others, you should agree with the main contractor about the provision of first aid. Put that agreement in writing and satisfy yourself that adequate provision is in fact made.

Each first-aid box should contain standard items including adhesive and other dressings, a triangular bandage, at least one sterile eye pad, and a guidance card or leaflet giving first-aid advice. If in doubt seek advice from EMAS (see p. 48). A qualified first-aider is always an asset, although it is not compulsory for small firms generally to have one unless there is a special hazard. Training has to be in accordance with official standards; and records, including dates of qualifications and refresher courses, should be kept. Also keep a record of treatments. An official Accident Book has to be kept available for employees to use.

Consider from the beginning what outside help (i.e. hospitals and doctors) is available locally. Post emergency telephone numbers up by the telephone in case of need. If there are no such facilities locally, increase your on-the-spot provision, and don't forget to check the first-aid boxes regularly!

Seating

This has to be considered under two headings:

1. Seats for regular use by employees who do their work seated (e.g. at a conveyor).
2. seats for occasional use, such as those provided for shop assistants to use when they are not serving customers.

Seats should be of suitable height and design for the individual and there should be adequate space (e.g. for handling material and moving about). People with physical disabilities should be catered for according to their needs.

All too often seats are not suitable for the particular operations; for instance, it is known that some of the stress felt by VDU operators may be traced back to unsuitable seating or their failing to adjust the chair properly.

6

the working environment

What is a suitable temperature? • What is good ventilation? • Lighting standards • Noise • Vibration • Stress • Good housekeeping

The working environment encompasses both physical and non-physical factors. People work best if they are reasonably comfortable at work. This depends largely on temperature, humidity, ventilation, lighting, noise and other characteristics of the physical environment. For most working environments, you have a large measure of control, and penny-pinching on such matters is a false economy.

Good working conditions promote a firm's interests. Attractive pictures sometimes hang on the walls of computer rooms and give the operators an opportunity to look at them to change the focus of their eyes from the screen, thus preventing undue eye-strain. Potted plants are not unknown but tend to be limited to the reception area where they give visitors a good impression and staff pleasant surroundings

You and your employees spend a significant part of your life in the working environment which you provide. Each has his or her individual 'microclimate' which affects health and well-being. Some are more sensitive to heat, cold, draughts and so on; some like working alone, others do not.

If you propose to install an open-plan office, bear this kind of thing in mind. Not everyone will appreciate its communal aspects and may feel under constant surveillance and miss the privacy which a small office or room provides. There are pros and cons to weigh up before making the decision. One aspect which is often overlooked is that fire spreads more easily in large unbroken spaces because barriers to fire spread are absent; even if partitions are used they may not be enough to hold back a fire which breaks out.

What is a suitable temperature?

The ideal temperature depends upon the nature of the work. The minimum temperature in workrooms for sedentary work is 16 degrees Celsius (about 60 degrees Fahrenheit). Where the work involves severe physical effort the minimum should be 13 degrees Celsius (about 55 degrees Fahrenheit). A sufficient number of thermometers should be placed around the working areas.

In some situations you have little or no control over the ambient temperature (e.g. work at ovens, furnaces and other hot plant; work inside cold stores and other cold places; outdoor work). For hot environments, do all you can to improve conditions by insulation, additional local ventilation or other means. Then – and for cold conditions – do what you can for the individual. Sometimes this means, for instance, that you have to provide insulating clothing and to arrange for extra work pauses. Weather protection by suitable clothing and huts or other shelter is generally needed for outdoor workers. Excessive humidity, especially if associated with a high temperature, is to be avoided indoors.

What is good ventilation?

Fresh air is required for several reasons as well as for respiration:

- to dilute airborne impurities like body odour, tobacco smoke (if permitted in the workplace), etc.
- to remove excess heat
- to dilute dusts, fumes and other process impurities

Adequate air movement is needed to provide a feeling of freshness without causing disagreeable draughts. Fresh air is distinguished from recirculated air such as is found in air-conditioning systems. These allow some impurities to build up which on occasion reach an unacceptable level.

Windows which open will often suffice. Where mechancial ventilation or air-conditioning is provided, it must be regularly and properly cleaned, tested and maintained.

Sick building syndrome

Minor illnesses like headaches and eye trouble are known to

affect people working in modern, well-sealed buildings with mechanical ventilation or air conditioning compared with workers in older, naturally ventilated ones. The term 'sick building syndrome' is applied to such conditions today but is not yet fully understood. Research is proceeding on this subject.

Legionnaire's disease

This was first identified in 1976 and appears as a form of pneumonia. The cause is a bacterium which is found in many recirculating and hot water systems such as those installed in large office blocks. Most outbreaks of the disease have been associated with hot water services and recirculating cooling water systems of air conditioning plant. These systems are often of poor design or badly maintained. Prevention is largely a technical matter and if you have an office in a large block, check with the owners that the maintenance, cleaning, testing and operating procedures are adequate. The bacteria responsible are no respecters of persons or places, and they have been found in the House of Commons recently according to newspaper reports.

Advice may be sought from a medical officer from the local authority or the director of the local public health laboratory. Any outbreak in England and Wales should be reported to a medical officer from the local authority or, in Scotland, to the Community Medicine Specialist and the HSE or Environmental Health Department of the local authority.

Humidifier fever

This illness is not the same as Legionnaire's disease, although both arise from the same source, i.e. contaminated water systems in buildings. It is a flu-like condition caused by the inhalation of fine droplets of water from humidifiers which have become contaminated. An example comes from the print industry where humidifiers are used to stabilise paper size and condition.

Prevention is by: choosing a suitable humidifier system (e.g. steam humidifier); maintaining it free from contamination by inspecting it weekly and taking care of its cleanliness.

If, in spite of your precautions, you have a problem, turn off the humidifier, notify a doctor and call in a ventilation specialist.

Lighting standards

Adequate and suitable lighting is needed:

- to enable people to see what they are doing and where they are going
- to illuminate potential hazards such as a hidden step
- to foster cleanliness
- to prevent eye strain

To be suitable, it should for instance also be free from glare, pools of darkness should be excluded, fluorescent lighting should not flicker, and excessive and sudden contrast should be avoided. To get the best out of your lighting system, keep light fittings clean and have a light-coloured ceiling to reflect the light.

An office worker left a brilliantly lit building one winter afternoon. As he did so and stepped into the poorly lighted yard where there were deep shadows, he was blinded for the moment, tripped over a low, flat truck, fell and fractured his skull.

Emergency lighting is not normally needed but is essential where its absence could lead to danger. For instance, if the normal lighting failed and this required that a process must be shut down immediately for safety reasons. It may also be needed to illuminate fire escape routes in some cases.

Noise

Measuring noise is a technical matter and the practical approach is first to decide whether you have a noise problem. If so, try and exclude, or at least reduce it, at source. Quieter machines are desirable and if you are purchasing plant, consider how much noise in use it produces. You could be buying a noise problem also, with the duty of dealing with it.

Loud noise can cause irreversible hearing damage and lead

to stress. Check on the noise levels in your places of work. A practical test is if you cannot hear someone clearly who is about 2 m away, the noise level is likely to be about 85dB(A) (i.e. decibels). Also check how long people are exposed to a lot of noise. Measurements of noise need to be done by a competent person however.

In some noisy places the statutory requirements for health supervision extend to health checks for employees who might be affected. The HSE considers these advisable when the sound levels reach 90dB(A) (i.e. decibels on the A-scale). Workplace measurements of noise are usually measured in terms of 'the sound pressure level' expressed in decibels on the A-weighted scale.

Precautions include minimising the amount and duration of noise (e.g. by engineering control such as acoustic enclosure), identifying and marking high noise zones and excluding persons who are not wearing hearing protection (which you should supply). Where necessary, rotate jobs so as to reduce individual exposure times.

Noise is a major health topic and many employees have reached retirement age with hearing impaired by their work. If you have a noise problem – and this should be revealed in your risk assessment – you need to take action. This may require the services of an expert. Portable noise meters are available but ensure that any you use are designed in accordance with British Standards and that you have a calibrator for use to check the meter's accuracy.

On buying new – or secondhand – plant, check on the noise emitted in use. In all cases, keep employees informed of the risk and the precautions. If they are concerned about their hearing, advise them to seek medical advice.

Vibration

The hazards of vibration present a real problem and the effects can be very harmful. Several types of injury or disease may be caused by prolonged exposure to high levels of local vibration (e.g. Vibration White Finger (VWF)). Tools associated with VWF include pneumatic hammers and other machines, hand-held portable grinders, chain saws and electrically-driven vibrating tools generally. Regular use of any of these may cause finger, hand and arm problems, in particular. Other effects have been recorded also. Seek expert help if you have a problem.

A man employed as gardener-handyman at a country house had to use a chain saw from time to time. For months he would not have to handle it then he might have to do so for several days running. After only 18 months' employment – and he was aged in his early thirties – he noticed that his hands felt numb and cold. He consulted a doctor who diagnosed VWF.

Stress

Stress is now recognised as having an important influence on people in all kinds of jobs and at all levels. The context in which people work may have a significant effect. Stress may be caused, for instance, by: the nature of the work (e.g. pressure of conveyor-belt working); the pace of working (e.g. to reach set targets); payment systems (e.g. incentive systems may lead to 'corner-cutting' in safety); repetition and monotony; shift work; the attitude of supervisors and managers (and perhaps yours); the behaviour of other employees; abuse of alcohol and drugs.

It is wise to bear such matters in mind for not everyone responds in the same way and stressed employees present a problem.

Teachers and welfare workers in contact with the public, for example, often suffer from stress-related health problems. Harassment, verbal abuse and even violence now menace them in their everyday work. Stress may also be caused by the manner in which their work is organised and managed. An overbearing manager or supervisor can undermine the success of a firm by demoralising their subordinates. Employers themselves need to ensure that they also do not cause stress in employees, however unintentionally.

Good housekeeping

This homely term has relevance in every workplace. It means cleanliness, tidiness and maintenance of the environment free from unnecessary risk. It is also an important fire precaution. Regular cleaning is an obvious need as is periodical redecoration – with extra careful hygiene where food is handled. It is necessary to keep premises free from such unwelcome visitors as cockroaches, not to mention rats and mice. Whilst floors are wet during cleaning, keep people away and put up a warning notice 'wet floor'. Avoid having trailing cables where people have to walk. Remove broken glass promptly. Even cabbage leaves left lying on the floor have caused workpeople to slip and get hurt. Records of redecoration should be kept for inspection.

Window cleaning

Window cleaning is needed regularly. You should be aware of the means of access to all windows. Roof windows, for example, may be awkward to reach and this could create safety problems. Windows in fragile roofs present a special danger and such roofs are deceptively fragile to walk or even stand on. For flat roofs, lightweight staging should be provided unless permanent walkways are installed. On sloping roofs well-secured roof ladders or crawling boards are needed. If you employ an outside firm of window cleaners make sure that you have done all you should to provide safe conditions for them and remind them of the need to work safely – you are paying them to do so.

7

fire precautions

*Fire as a serious danger • What are the possible sources
of ignition? • What is fuel for a fire? • Is fire detection
apparatus necessary? • What about fire fighting? • Is
security relevant?*

Fire as a serious danger

Fires can put you out of business temporarily – or
permanently. They even gobble up your business papers and
records. They obviously damage property and unfortunately
sometimes lead to serious, even fatal, injuries. Your first
objective is to prevent it happening; but you also need to
consider how to deal with a fire – before it happens. A fire
needs: a source of ignition to start it; a fuel to start and
sustain it; oxygen to support combustion; sufficient temperature to keep it going.

All these factors are present in indoor places of work and
often outdoors. They provide the clues to fire precautions
generally.

What are the possible sources of ignition?

Common ones are:

- electricity
- smouldering cigarette ends
- open flames
- matches
- heaters

Electric installations should be suitable for the work; for
example, for some processes, flameproof equipment is
needed. All repairs and modifications to the system should
be done by a qualified electrician. In due course, the complete installation will need to be replaced, so have it tested
periodically.

It is up to you, at the present time, whether to allow tobacco smoking on the premises. If you do, you will need to control it by confining it to certain areas and times (see Chapter 5). But this still allows a potential source of ignition to be present which you could avoid. In some cases, as where highly flammable or radioactive substances are used, smoking is prohibited.

Open flames from gas burners and welding apparatus are examples of common ignition sources. Matches which are thrown away at the workplace may be still alight, thus creating a further hazard. Electric radiant heaters too can cause fires to start.

In one small factory, a radiant heater was placed in the cloakroom to dry the employees' clothing which was wet. The heat dried the nearest clothing, the localised temperature then rose and suddenly some overheated clothing burst into flame. The factory was badly damaged.

What is fuel for a fire?

Almost anything will burn if the temperature is high enough. Fires start with any material which acts as tinder when ignited. Highly flammable materials are legion. Examples are: liquids such as solvents and oils; solids such as loose paper and polyurethane foam; fumes and gases such as acetylene and LP gas.

The first rule is to use the safest materials that you can, then to have the minimum amount on the premises which enables work to proceed. The bulk should be stored away from the building in a suitable place. For the storage of petroleum and certain petroleum products, a licence to store is needed from the local authority. Post a clear warning notice outside the store. In the workroom, keep the main supplies in a closed metal cupboard or bin, duly labelled on the outside. Use safety containers at the process, if possible, and control any spillage by the method of work (e.g. over a tray). Inform and train your employees.

Good housekeeping should ensure that loose paper, cardboard, plastics and other flammables do not lie about. Be aware of less obvious risks such as hydrogen gas, which is flammable and is given off from battery charging (e.g. for your fork-lift truck). Another matter often overlooked is that a so-called 'empty' drum which has contained a flammable liquid is still quite dangerous. Do not apply heat to it; dispose of it safely.

Gas cylinders

Many cylinders contain flammable gas (e.g. acetylene gas) and need to be stored, handled and used with care. Never store cylinders of heavy gas below ground level as any escaping gas can creep into places, thus presenting a further risk. If you are a regular user of gases at particular points, as in a laboratory, it is advisable to keep the gas cylinders in a safe compound outside, and pipe in the gases through permanent piping. Good ventilation is also necessary.

Cylinders should be protected from damage by chaining them onto suitable trolleys. If you need the cylinders on an upper floor, check that they are carried safely either by lift or by two men.

Is fire detection apparatus necessary?

If there is a fire, the sooner you know, the better. Install suitable fire detection apparatus but seek advice as to the type suited to your conditions. Your nose is also a useful auxiliary detector – never ignore a smell of burning.

A fire alarm which is linked to the fire station is likely to bring the fire brigade more quickly than a telephone call – people sometimes delay telephoning, because they underrate the danger, panic or misunderstand instructions.

In one department store, the telephone operator misheard the panicky tone of the manager who had detected a fire. She thought he said something else when he actually said: 'There is a fire!'. This led to several minutes' delay in calling the fire brigade – and a bigger fire.

When fires grow to disastrous levels, the cause is invariably either that they were not discovered in time or that they could not be successfully fought with the means available – personnel and equipment. The object is to detect the fire within a few minutes of its breaking out. There are various types of detection apparatus.

The fire alarm itself should have a distinctive sound and should not, for instance, be a particular number of rings on the 'stop work' bell. It should be audible throughout the building. However inconvenient it is to stop work and vacate the premises when the bell sounds, you should always heed it. A problem can arise with oversensitive bells which produce a lot of false alarms. If you have such a one, get it rectified immediately.

At a university there was an oversensitive fire alarm bell. The academics and others became annoyed at the too frequent interruption of their work, so the practice grew up of ignoring it. Some did obey its call only to be laughed at by students and staff grinning from upper windows. Yet, if a fire *does* in fact occur in that building, no one may be sure if it is real and this may result in fatality.

Have a plan of action for reacting to any fire which is detected and check the fire alarm every week: you may need it in a hurry one day.

What about fire fighting?

The sooner a fire is tackled, the better. On site, fire extinguishing equipment may put out a small fire, if properly used, but is more likely to 'hold the fort' until the fire brigade arrives. People should not expose themselves to danger in fighting a fire, and employees should be trained in the use of the equipment.

The kind of apparatus you need (e.g. fire extinguishers) requires some expert advice, for example, from the fire brigade. Install the right kind and number in suitable places where they are always readily accessible. They will need to be inspected regularly and refilled as necessary. In a kitchen a fire blanket is useful.

Training

The need to receive training and 'hands-on' experience with fire fighting apparatus of any kind is real. This has to be arranged by you. The fire brigade may be willing to offer instruction if sufficient numbers of people are interested. If you share a building with others, they, too, should share in this. The worst time to learn how to operate apparatus is after a fire has broken out. Fires should be tackled immediately, not when you have had time to put on your glasses and pore over the small print on the labels on fire extinguishers – which are not all the same, incidentally.

A memorable demonstration took place on a supervisors' course on general management which included fire fighting. Unfortunately, the fire brigade member who usually came to give this demonstration could not do so, and the lecturer decided to do it himself. After all, he had seen the fireman do it on previous courses ... He started confidently, but the fire extinguisher nozzle took the initiative, gyrated above his head, discharging the energy stored up in the appliance. He struggled in vain to take control and only succeeded when the appliance had expended its contents. The trainees found this a refreshing change from the rest of the course and no doubt, whatever else they have forgotten, the memory of this remains with them.

Fire spread

Once it has started, a fire can rip through the premises if you give it the right opportunity. Layout can be used to limit fire spread in various ways such as: isolate processes where highly flammable substances are used; use barriers (e.g. fire-resisting walls); avoid congestion of materials; keep doors closed at flammable-material cupboards; keep the premises and plant clean; clear deposits in dust extractors; remove grease from kitchen ventilators and cooker hoods.

If you have some heavy machinery, locate it on the ground floor. If there is a fire which damages the structure sufficiently, heavy equipment is liable to crash through the ceiling.

Fire escape

Everyone in the building – visitors as well as employees – should be able to escape in case of fire, quickly and easily.

Unless your firm is extremely small you will need a fire certificate from the local fire authority, so apply for one. This will be issued, certifying your escapes, once you have met their requirements.

All escape routes should be kept unobstructed. This seems obvious but may be overlooked.

One small Midlands company had just received a consignment of drums of flammable material but could not find sufficient space to store it. Then the manager had a brain wave and remembered that there was one quiet, unused space ... the external fire escape. This is where the Factory Inspector found the drums.

The fire exit doors should be clearly marked and kept closed. They should never be propped open – no, not even by a fire extinguisher! You may need a copy of your part of a fire certificate if you are one of a number of occupants of a sizeable building. Check this with the owner who should hold the certificate for the building.

Fire drills are highly desirable though rarely popular. Make sure everyone, including the newest recruit, knows how to get out in case of fire. Remember that there will be smoke and perhaps nasty fumes in a real fire. Consider also the safety of visitors to your premises. Once people are out of the building they should gather at a muster point for checking, so as to ensure that no one is left in the building.

Is security relevant?

Taking precautions against fire may – but usually need not – lead to security problems.

In a 13-storey building in the centre of a major city, the occupiers locked the ground floor fire exit because they feared that vandals might enter and create some havoc. The answer was to provide a door which could be readily opened from inside but not from outside.

8

dangerous materials

*What is a dangerous substance? • Modes of attack •
Inhalation • Permits to work • Swallowing • Skin contact •
Labelling • Other modes of attack • Precautions
•Flammables • Sources of information*

New substances, new products and new processes can lead
to new hazards which you need to be aware of if they are
used or stored in your firm. The primary safeguard is to use
the safest material you can even if it is not the cheapest.

Substances harmful to health are legion, ranging from
solvents to agricultural pesticides, from cyanides to mercury
– and many, many more.

What is a dangerous substance?

It might be said that no substance is safe in all its forms.
Even water – for it can scald and engulf people who fall into
it. In more homely terms, a dangerous substance is one
which has the potential for harming people's health. This it
may do immediately as when someone is overcome by a gas
like carbon monoxide (as emitted by car exhausts), or it may
create deferred or chronic effects (for instance, lead may be
built up in the body until a point is reached where lead
poisoning manifests itself).

For any dangerous substance you have to make an assessment of the risk. The term 'hazard' in this context refers to
the potential for harm and the term 'risk' refers to the
likelihood that it will cause harm in the actual circumstances
of use.

You have first to assess the risk to people's health as a
result of the way a particular substance is used or stored in
your business. You then have to decide what safeguards are
needed. Effective controls have to be established, your
workforce has to be trained and informed as necessary and
you need to monitor the situation to ensure that no harm
results. In some cases, medical surveillance will be needed.

There are five key steps in carrying out the assessment:

1. Gather information about the substance, the work and working practices.
2. Identify the hazards and evaluate the risks to health.
3. Decide what needs to be done to prevent or control exposure.
4. Take suitable action without delay.
5. Record your assessment unless, for example, there is no risk found.
6. Review the assessment after a suitable time.

As a result, set in motion whatever precautions are needed.

Modes of attack

It is useful in practice to know by what means a substance harms the body. At the risk of oversimplification, there are three main modes:

- inhalation
- swallowing
- skin contact

Inhalation

A wide range of dusts, fumes, gases and vapours is given off in various processes. If inhaled, they lead to lung diseases and other harm. Dust is produced not only in manufacturing but in work such as rubbing down a lead-painted surface preparatory to repainting.

It has been said that many small firms simply fail to recognise health risks in their undertakings. For instance, occupational asthma is a growing problem and is associated with the use of a range of substances. Such risks should be identified in risk assessments which have to be carried out.

Publicity has been given in the media about that silent killer, carbon monoxide. Burning gas in circumstances where there is inadequate ventilation and hence a shortage of oxygen can lead to this insidious gas being formed. This risk also occurs in flats, houses and elsewhere.

Two young women lost their lives in a caravan on a farm where they were staying and a third one became unconscious but survived. The fixed ventilation and defective flueing arrangements for the gas heater led to the formation of carbon monoxide (CO) which they inhaled.

Asbestos

Special controls are needed when asbestos, lead or carcinogenic (cancer-producing) substances are used. There are special regulations for these substances.

There are different kinds of asbestos including crocidolite which is called blue asbestos. In practice, care must be taken with all kinds of asbestos dust. If you encounter asbestos in your business you will need to seek specialised advice. Asbestos presents a serious breathing risk and this points to the type of precautions needed to prevent the dust entering the breathing air (e.g. containment and exhaust appliances). You also have to take great care in the disposing of asbestos.

Only contractors licensed by HSE may lawfully work on certain asbestos work such as insulation and coating and they have to comply with strict safety conditions, including those relating to waste disposal.

Less obvious processes where asbestos dust may present a danger include: grinding brake linings and cleaning brake assemblies in repair garages; removing insulation from old buildings in demolition work – and cleaning floors in any premises where there is liable to be asbestos dust.

An unexpected encounter with blue asbestos took place when a firm was asked to renovate an Armstrong Siddeley car built in the 1930s. The vehicle body panels, floor and bulkheads had been lined with blue asbestos. A specialist asbestos removal contractor was – rightly – called in to do the work.

Owners of pre-war, veteran and vintage cars are warned!

Lead

Another widely used material which is met in various forms is lead. Like asbestos, it is subject to strict regulations. The main risk is inhalation but it may also be swallowed (e.g. if someone eats a sandwich without washing their hands first). Lead is a cumulative poison and like all insidious diseases can too easily be ignored.

Lead is used in a multitude of work activities such as: use of lead compounds producing dust, as in battery manufacture; firing small firearms in indoor ranges; spraying lead paint; working inside tanks which have contained leaded petrol, as in oil terminals; lead emission when testing petrol engines, as in garages.

Organic solvents

Many kinds of solvents are commonly used in industry and other places of work such a perchloroethylene in dry cleaning and trichloroethylene in processes such as degreasing.

A major research programme is under way to study the possibility of a link between occupational exposure to perchloroethylene and a suspected increase of miscarriages among women who work in dry cleanmg where it is used as a cleaning agent. Until the findings are completed and published, employers are urged to tighten precautions so that concentrations are below the Occupational Exposure Standards (see below), and to prevent skin contact with perchloroethylene.

A director of a newly-established company was working on his own when he went into a standard degreasing tank with the express intention of checking the bottom of the tank. There were only a few gallons of trichloroethylene there, but they were sufficient to cause him to be overcome. He collapsed and died before help arrived.

This illustrates the danger of entering a tank even when only a very small amount of solvent is present. Even if there is only sludge and the tank appears to be empty, the feet stir this up and release gas. Other solvents present similar hazards.

Pesticides

Pesticides used in crop spraying are a matter of concern not only for farm workers but also for members of the public when it drifts in their direction. In about 50 per cent of cases investigated in 1994/95, it was alleged that ill-health had been caused to someone and the number of cases has increased recently. Crop spraying can be done safely if the best practice is always followed but do not spray at all unless it is essential – and always choose the safest material for the job.

A teacher was giving a sports lesson in the playing field of a school to 50 children when he noted a strange taste in his mouth. A machine was spraying pesticides merrily in an adjoining field and the wind had caused spray to drift towards them.

Farm workers also face possible health risks when undertaking sheep dipping. The HSE has issued recommendations for farmers on the subject which include: decide if you really need to dip; if so, use the product best suited not only to prevent and control parasites but also to minimise risks to personnel and reduce risks to the environment and to you.

Occupational exposure limits

The term OES means Occupational Exposure Standard which, subject to certain conditions, refers to the concentration of an airborne substance which, according to current knowledge, is unlikely to cause injury to health. The figures are revised as necessary as new information is available. Official tables are issued and updated. This is distinct from MEL which refers to the Maximum Exposure Limit allowed for a substance. The aim should always be to minimise exposure and never to exceed the OES.

COSHH

This acronym has done wonders for publicity. It stands for the Control of Substances Hazardous to Health and the regulations have been consolidated recently.

Three workers in a bicycle factory were employed to dip parts into industrial methylated spirits to remove dust. They then had to apply an epoxy resin adhesive with a small spatula. But the precautions were inadequate and all of them suffered skin disease as a result

---

Permits to work

Where work has to be done inside any tank, pit, pipe or similar confined space where there is a risk of being overcome by fumes, gases or vapours, a 'permit-to-work' system may have to be used. This is a written system of authorisation signed by a responsible member of management allowing someone to enter the confined space under specified conditions.

The first step is to remove sources of the dangerous material (e.g. the liquid and sludge), then care has to be taken to prevent their ingress, and the space has to be properly ventilated. After satisfying himself or herself by testing that the space is safe to enter without breathing apparatus, the authorised person may issue the written permit to a particular member of staff, specifying the time limit to be spent inside the tank. If breathing apparatus has to be worn, the permit will say so and this must be of approved type. Where practicable, the person entering the tank must also wear a belt with attached rope, the end of which is held by a person outside capable of pulling the worker out in case of need. All the necessary equipment must be provided and this also includes suitable reviving apparatus which must be kept in good condition.

A tank had contained a substance which had been cleared out by feeding a solvent to it and draining it off several times. A check suggested that the original substance had been fully removed. As an extra precaution, the manhole cover was then left off for some hours for any fumes to dissipate. Then a workman leant into the tank probably to recover a tool he had dropped into it. He was overcome by fumes and never regained consciousness. A proper 'permit-to-work' system would have saved his life.

All the persons involved must be trained in the work they have to do and a sufficient number of people must be practised in the use of the apparatus, including that used for resuscitation.

Printed forms are used for permits, not scraps of paper. If you propose to do work involving entry into confined spaces you will need to seek advice first. Where an outside contractor is involved, precautions must be fully observed by them also.

In one case a contracting firm was doing work inside tanks for a big oil company. This company had very strict rules with a 'permit-to-work' system and required the contractors to observe them in detail. Noticing that one of the contractor's men was about to enter a tank with his breathing apparatus slung over his shoulder instead of being worn, the oil company stopped the man and caused him to be disciplined severely for this breach of safety rules.

Swallowing

Poisons may be conveyed to the mouth as in the case of lead. The precautions are, firstly, to minimise the risk of contact with the poison concerned but always accept that there is liable to be some on the hands. Care is needed and this requires careful washing. For this purpose, you have to provide good washing facilities, including warm water, soap and nail brushes. The workers must use them before eating food or going home. This means that you have to provide facilities for them to eat away from the workplace. Discipline is necessary to ensure that the precautions are followed.

Never put dangerous liquid substances into milk or squash bottles, or jam jars. Liquids should be kept in proper containers, labelled with their contents. Manufacturers supply their products duly labelled also with the dangers and necessary precautions listed.

The workshop of a small factory was littered with mostly-empty lemonade bottles. But there were a few partly full and this served as an inspiration for a practical joker among the men. He added some trichloroethylene to one of these and waited for a workmate to come along to slake his thirst. This happened and the unfortunate man was taken to hospital and detained for a week. This illustrated not only the danger of unlabelled bottles, but also the responsibility management has to prevent horseplay. It was also an indictment of the standard of 'housekeeping' there.

Skin contact

Individuals vary in their susceptibility to skin complaints when in contact with chemicals and other materials. Many substances attack the skin such as: mineral oils, soluble cutting oils, paraffin, white spirit, solvents generally and certain kinds of wood dust as well as the host of chemicals. Ordinary substances like flour can cause skin problems which are generally classed as occupational dermatitis.

The danger of overexposing the skin to sunlight is important today. All outdoor workers, such as those who work on farms, building sites and in market gardens, should heed the warning. The skin should be protected by clothing including wide-brimmed hats to shade the face, head and back of neck.

There are risks attending the use of sun-beds and other tanning equipment such as is used for cosmetic purposes. Operators have a duty to provide safety information to their customers. Excessive exposure to the ultra-violet radiation can cause serious skin problems which may not be apparent for some time.

Labelling

Modern regulations have highlighted the need for careful and full labelling of dangerous substances. They require that certain terms are used more precisely for such purposes.

Drums and other containers of dangerous substances, under specific legislation, have to carry labels with hazard warning symbols and what are called 'guidance phrases'. These are:

- R-phrases such as 'toxic by inhalation' and 'irritating to the eyes'
- S-phrases such as 'keep away from heat' and 'avoid contact with the skin'

The R-phrases thus refer to the nastier properties of the substance whilst the S-phrases give advice as to precautions to be taken.

All firms use dangerous substances, if only for cleaning purposes, so attention is drawn to the labels which are placed on them. If you produce dangerous substances, you will need to seek advice about the details of the regulations relating to the labelling of your products before despatch.

Train your staff also to read labels and endeavour to ensure that labels are not obliterated as the contents of containers dribble over the side. Sometimes leaflets are provided by manufacturers or suppliers to give information and advice. Keep these for reference and refer to them.

Other modes of attack

There is also a miscellaneous and important group of diseases which can be suffered e.g. in: work with ionising radiations; work involving ultra-violet radiation; work involving infra-red radiation; work with the soil; work involving possible contact with rats' urine.

Precautions

Much has already been indicated about the necessary precautions which have to be geared to the nature of the particular danger. A check list of common precautions may be useful at this stage, although not all will be pertinent to every substance. There is one overriding precaution, however. Always use the safest material that you can. Key precautions are:

- keep the minimum quantities on site
- keep the minimum quantities in the workplace itself
- store the remainder safely
- learn about the dangers – 'know your enemy'
- provide proper plant (e.g. suitable vacuum cleaners)
- provide suitable ventilation (e.g. mechanical extraction)
- maintain all plant and equipment
- incorporate safety into the methods of work
- use a 'permit-to-work' system
- train your employees in safe working
- monitor your employees' work for safety
- use disciplinary measures to enforce safety
- plan the layout to minimise dangers
- enclose dangerous substances as much as possible
- dispose of waste properly
- avoid discharging harmful substances into the atmosphere
- provide washing facilities of the requisite standard
- provide a place for eating food away from the workplace
- prohibit smoking where there is dangerous material

- provide protective clothing
- arrange for the storage and cleaning of protective clothing
- provide breathing apparatus or other suitable protection
- provide personal protection (e.g. safety helmets)
- provide barrier creams against skin problems
- observe the manufacturer's recommendations
- provide advice on dangerous materials which you supply to others

This list is not exhaustive and you will need to select those items which apply to your work. It will be a relief to know that you are unlikely to have to comply with them all in one small firm.

Flammables

There are many substances which are dangerous because they are flammable and/or explosive. The dust of many everyday substances can form explosive dust clouds in certain conditions. Examples are: wood, cork, grain, sugar, certain metals (e.g magnesium) and some plastics.

Flammable gases, fumes and vapours include those given off by such materials as: LP gas, benzene, acetone, carbon monoxide, ether, methane, and petroleum spirit ('petrol').
Petrol is dangerous both as a liquid and a vapour, and may harm the skin. Neither it nor substances like paraffin should ever be used to brighten fires as this is extremely dangerous.

A self-employed car sprayer was clearing out a railway arch prior to leasing it for his vehicle-repair business. So he borrowed a 182-litre (40-gallon) drum to burn waste from the neighbouring premises. This contained some smouldering material to get a fire going. He walked over to the drum with a 23-litre (5-gallon) can of petroleum thinners – in which he had punctured some holes ready for a nice fire – and started to brighten the fire with the thinners. But Nemesis overtook him: he got his good fire but also an explosion in which he suffered 60 per cent burns.

Spontaneous combustion of rags soaked in some flammable materials can take place without warning if contaminated with certain flammable solvents. Flammable materials of many sorts have contributed to the known accidents.

An industrial painter was painting the inside of a pipe about 1.37 m (4 ft 6 in) in diameter, situated on a hillside with a slope of 1 in 4. An LP gas-powered lamp, used for lighting the work, was accidentally knocked over, rolled along and set fire to a paint tray which contained some bitumen paint. This was flammable with a flash point of about 32°C. The painter tried to escape past the flames but his paint-soaked overalls were ignited. Under the contract the painter's employer should have provided low voltage flameproof lighting. This would have prevented ignition.

Substances which are both dangerous to health and flammable include some of those already named such as carbon monoxide which can form an explosive mixture with air. Solvents generally attack the skin of susceptible people. In short, flammable materials are dangerous and all too often they also pose a danger to health.

Sources of information

One point which must emerge very clearly from consideration of dangerous materials is that you will be asking where you can obtain the necessary information. Sources of information include: labels and leaflets supplied with the products; the manufacturers and suppliers directly; the HSE directly; the local environmental health department; HSE publications; trade associations; trade publications; safety consultants.

It is also hoped that this book will provide some of the answers.

EMAS

Medical advice may be needed and the Employment Medical Advisory Service (EMAS) offers specialised advice and information of a medical nature. They are linked with the HSE and may be contacted directly or through the HSE.

9

are your products safe?

*Faults in work equipment • Faults in domestic equipment •
Articles for use at work • Substances for use at work •
Waste • Erection and installation of plant*

From tentative beginnings in the older safety statute, the
Factories Act, there has been a blossoming of criminal product
safety legislation. Originally, only a few named dangerous
parts of machinery had to be safeguarded before being sold or
hired out. Today the liability is considerably deeper and wider.
More employers and undertakings generally have duties and
those duties have expanded considerably.

In addition, the growing consumer safety legislation has
now been closely linked with that for health and safety at
work and they have to be seen as a whole.

Faults in work equipment

Because of the link between suppliers and their customers,
defects are likely to be dealt with directly between the
parties and receive little publicity. But many products are
used both in a work situation and in the home, and
advertisements draw attention to the need to take action
(e.g. return the product to the manufacturers). Thus a
washing machine designed primarily for the domestic
market may be used by hairdressers. Other recent examples
have been: an extension lead which was found to be
dangerous in certain circumstances; certain imported
chargers for mobile telephones, chain saws; power drills
and jig saws. Usually it is only certain identifiable models
which are at fault and these are clearly indicated in any
publicity.

Faults in domestic equipment

Advertisements in newspapers are an important way in which defects of domestic products are brought to public notice. They cover many items and the following is a selection of real cases: faulty control device in electrical equipment which could lead to a lethal fire; defective installation of certain central heating boilers; defect in bottom bracket axle of bicycle; risk of severe overheating in microwave oven; parts flying off a garden machine; on/off switch of TV set which can deteriorate rapidly and overheat so as to cause fire; welding weakness in handlebar of tricycles; freestanding cooker liable to topple over if door open and heavy load imposed on it.

Products for children are sometimes defective. Warnings have been issued about a child's ball and about a cot because a possible safety problem could arise. A magnanimous women's journal gave away children's rattles and then had to recall them, postage paid, because it was found that they might fracture in certain circumstances. But not all domestic dangers are immediately foreseeable as in the case of one lady with a Yorkshire zeal for hygiene. She was reported as having fallen into her wheelie bin when cleaning it.

Articles designed for use at work are dealt with differently when users are known. They are contacted directly, as are the manufacturers.

Before you as an employer feel reassured by this, it should be made clear that employers are still liable for the safety in the place of work however much at fault the manufacturer or others might be. As an employer you have duties to perform and if someone else is also at fault, this does not exempt you from your responsibilities. You both have to conform.

Persons liable

For safety at work, the duties are encapsulated in a section of the 1974 Act which is as laborious to read as it is important to understand. Some basic details need to be explained first.

To save constant repetition, the references are mainly to manufacturers but others have similar duties. These are designers, importers, suppliers and, with fewer duties, those who erect and install articles for use at work. The term 'suppliers' includes those who supply products by way of sale, lease, hire or hire-purchase (but not the finance companies dealing with hire-purchase), whether as a principal or an agent for another. If, for instance, your business is hiring out building plant, it is your job to check it for safety. When you hire it out again it should be in a safe condition.

Products

This is a convenient term which includes articles and substances for use at work. An 'article' in this sense means any plant such as machinery, equipment, appliance or components, designed for use at work even if it is used for other purposes too. There are no size limitations and an article might be a massive machine or a hammer for instance. In one recorded case, a number of imported mains tester screwdrivers were found to be faulty and potentially dangerous. In another case imported first-aid kits were found to be contaminated.

A 'substance for use at work' means any natural or artificial substance whether in solid or liquid form or in the form of gas or vapour, intended for use at work. As in the case of articles, substances do not need to be designed exclusively for use at work. It will be noted that the substances do not have to be dangerous ones as discussed in Chapter 8: *all substances are included.*

It is convenient to consider articles and substances separately although the requirements are generally in parallel. Products should comply with relevant British Standards.

Articles for use at work

The duties of the manufacturer and others are: to ensure that articles are safe and without risk to health; to subject articles to testing and examination; to undertake any necessary research; to provide users with adequate information.

Ensuring safety

The standard is one of reasonable practicability, unless specific requirements are laid down (e.g. in legislation). This means that the danger has to be assessed and set against the cost in terms of money and practical difficulties involved. If you decide that a particular safeguard is not reasonably practicable, you must be able to justify your decision if challenged.

A 40-feet-long earth scraper vehicle caused a fatal accident and much consternation on a motorway when it charged driverless out of control. It had been restarted by its driver ready for refuelling from a visiting tanker. As the driver started it up, he was beckoned by the foreman so he switched off one engine leaving the one which drove the scraper running. On his return he found that the starter-motor would not operate. He tried the drill for a stubborn refusal to start: he agitated the gear-lever to and fro then, unsuccessful, he started the motor by shorting the starter solenoid. The scraper immediately lurched forward and ran driverless from bank to bank. Another driver tried to climb into the cab but fell under one of the large front wheels and was killed instantly.

The official report after the investigation of the accident pointed out that there was a patent weakness in design in that such a large and sophisticated machine should depend for efficient operation on a flimsy and inadequate microswitch.

Testing and examination

This is necessary to ensure safety in use and much of it will take place at the production stage. Sometimes this work will already have been done elsewhere and the results will have been published. If you wish to rely on them, you need to satisfy yourself that they are appropriate and acceptable so as to relieve you of the need to repeat the testing and examination. Suppliers and importers may rely on manufacturers' data and will need to justify this decision if challenged. Those who lack facilities may use outside laboratories and test centres for the purpose.

Research

Any necessary research has to be done by designers and manufacturers with the objectives of (1) discovering any risks associated with the basic design and (2) eliminating or minimising them. Reliance may sometimes be placed on research carried out by others, for example: safe working loads; need for built-in safeguards; adequacy of the electrical earthing; methods of noise control; safe operating speed; specific precautions.

Information

The user will need adequate information about hazards and precautions and has to pass it on to employees. It is important that additional information is provided on request without delay. Sometimes information is best conveyed by an operating manual or even a leaflet. These should be written in clear language and cover the important items such as cleaning and maintenance as well as operating. Line drawings are often useful.

The purpose for which the article was designed should be made clear and instructions given regarding such matters as: how to operate, set, adjust and clean it; emergency arrangements (e.g. rapid shut-down); regular maintenance; periodic testing and replacement of components; safe working practices, use of protective equipment.

Risks have to be considered in the light of foreseeability which means that you have to keep up to date with information about the dangers of products which you supply and similar goods produced by others. Ignorance is no excuse. You should notify your customers when a new risk comes to light. This means contacting your business purchasers directly and advertising in the newspapers when you have to warn domestic customers or others not on your customer list who may be using the product in question.

Transfer of responsibilities

Some obligations may, under strict conditions, be transferred. This applies, for instance, if a customer wants an article made to his specifications such as unfinished plant. But he must give a written undertaking to the other party that he will provide the necessary safeguards.

Substances for use at work

The duties under this heading are those of manufacturers, importers and suppliers. They are broadly similar to those already outlined for articles for use at work. One practical difference is that whereas with plant it is known what it is to be used for, generally this is not so for substances (e.g. a chemical substance can be used for a multitude of purposes).

Information about the substance's properties should be provided (e.g. toxicity, flammability, explosibility, reactions with other materials, etc.). Information should also be given about the precautions which should be taken (e.g. recommended handling procedures, conditions of use to be avoided, etc.). The user should be supplied with any additional information as required.

Waste

It is not always realised that if you dispose of waste or waste products, or sell machinery second-hand you become a supplier subject to the same regulations. If re-use is not intended, the official advice is that this should be clearly stated in the contract of sale. If a substance is sold in a condition unfit for use this should similarly be documented. Modern environmental legislation applies to the handling and disposal of waste and this is a matter which you need to bear in mind.

Erection and installation of plant

Those who erect and install plant have to do so safely so that nothing in the way in which they do so creates a hazard. The case illustrated below shows how careful tradesmen and others now have to be.

An electrician was convicted of manslaughter after a young father was killed by electric shock at his kitchen sink. The electrician had wrongly wired the electrical equipment for the central heating system.

This was a landmark case and the position now is that tradesmen and others need to beware.

10

manual handling

Introduction • Risk assessment • Precautions •
Lifting techniques • Protective wear

Introduction

Injuries from manual handling are many and while most are sprains and strains, far too many are serious and may be permanently disabling. Some injuries are cumulative rather than caused solely by a single incident but have built up after years of handling loads. 'Manual handling' means any transporting or supporting of a load including the lifting, putting down, pushing, pulling, carrying or moving by hand or by bodily force or trying to do so.

Many of the injuries are caused to the back but other parts of the body may be affected (e.g. hands, arms, legs, feet or torso). Fatal injuries are rare but long-term damage is not. In the past, safety legislation dealt inadequately, even ignorantly, with the problem and limited itself largely to the weight of loads. This simplistic approach has long been discredited although the weight of a load remains one of the factors to be taken into account in assessing risk.

Risk assessment

This is intended to reveal the problems in your workplace and a record should be kept. It should point the way to necessary precautions. Remember that those who work away from base also have to be considered.

In undertaking a risk assessment the following items need to be considered:

- the nature of the task
- the load
- the working environment
- individual capability

In assessing the task consider whether the load – whatever it is – is held close to the body or perhaps at arm's length. In the latter case, the weight which can be safely handled is less. Is the spine twisted when under load? This can be very harmful indeed. Both excessive vertical or horizontal movements should be avoided. Storing things on high shelves for instance requires reaching up, grasping, holding and carrying the load and should be avoided where possible. Heavy files stored in offices contravene this safety standard if they have to be manhandled.

The load itself may present special problems to handlers. Loads come in all shapes and size and may be hard to grasp or hold. Nurses, who have to lift and move patients, suffer many back injuries but careful training and the observation of this teaching prevent many injuries. If you operate premises where there are patients, you should eliminate the risks by design (e.g. of bed heights) although good training remains essential.

The work environment encompasses both physical and non-physical aspects. The handling is made more difficult in hot and humid conditions or where there is poor lighting. In cold rooms in which people work and where frozen foods are stored manual handling is more difficult, especially where the lighting is liable to be dim and partly obscured. Slippery and overcrowded floors, ramps, steps and other impediments to free and level movement make handling more onerous.

Non-physical aspects can include such things as the pressure that employees working on piece rate payment systems are placed under if this pressure leads them to twist or strain themselves under loads in the course of hurrying to complete a task. Machine pacing (i.e. when the employee has to keep up with a machine relentlessly pouring out products for handling) also leads to haste which may be excessive. This is the negation of ergonomics which, in essence, means that the work should be fitted to the worker, not vice versa.

You will note what is being handled, the means used, the distance of travel (vertically and horizontally). The person doing the job and its frequency should also be considered.

The load may be a container of any kind, a machine, a sack of material, a lump of rubber, a number of bricks – or anything other than a tool being used for its intended purpose. You will note its dimensions (e.g. wide loads are more difficult to hold and the safe weight for handling is less; if it is wet, slippery or hot or has sharp edges, handling is more difficult).

The distance of travel is important and you should check the state of the floor or ground for unevenness, slipperiness and obstructions. Note the physical working environment, particularly lighting, humidity, high or low temperature (e.g. when men work in deep freezers in the food industry).

Noise can cause stress in this work as can excessive pressure of work, not least when being paced by a machine. Consider the individual's capacity for this work. The young man demonstrating his strength often – eventually – becomes the older man finding some lifting and carrying a strain. What techniques are employees using? Have they been trained in safe methods?

Precautions

The assessment should point the way to the action needed. The first precaution is to eliminate manual handling if possible and if it is not, to minimise it. This may be done, for example, by altering the layout, ceasing to store things on high shelves or too low down, stacking in a different way, changing the load. The means to be adopted depend on what you have found. If possible, mechanical handling should be substituted. This is the way of the future as fewer people will want to be packhorses.

Posture when handling goods should not require the arms to be outstretched or the spine twisted at the same time. Posture is often influenced by layout such as low headroom or floor obstructions or inadequate space.

The load may need to be altered, for example, split up to smaller size if the weight is excessive; or narrowed if too wide; provided with handles to give a better grip. Maybe a different container is advisable?

Check on the individual's training in lifting techniques if they appear to be incorrect and hence liable to cause injury. How much handling does the individual do in a day, a week? Injuries may result from cumulative strain.

In a three-star hotel the young receptionist was carrying a tray of tea down a spiral stairway to the front office. She held the tray in one hand as it was light in weight but, missing her footing, she tumbled to the bottom of the stairs. Her injuries included multiple fractures and scalding. Yet the accident could have been avoided by a suitable handrail.

Improvements are taking place although a great deal remains to be done. Conveyors reduce the carrying distance for human effort although the loading and unloading sometimes impose undesirable manhandling activity.

An industry in which improvements have been made and continue to be made is the drinks industry although some difficult problems remain; for example where there are 'difficult' drops at premises where the draymen have to face unloading problems which are difficult to eliminate. Where the breweries own the premises they have a better opportunity of improving conditions (e.g. by use of lifting appliances or by structural change).

Joint lifting

When two or more persons are lifting jointly, they should act in unison, with the load equally shared between them and one of them should act as leader to co-ordinate their joint effort. All should use basic safe lifting techniques and, if possible, they should be of similar height and build.

In one small works, liquid was drawn off a vessel near floor level into a bucket, then carried some 6m (20 ft) and lifted up to a bench where it was manipulated before being lifted again and carried to a machine some 3m (10 ft) away, then back to the bench, then to another machine about 3.6m (12 ft) away, then back to the bench before final operations making it ready for carrying to another area for packing. A lot of this manual handling could have been eliminated by better layout and all of it by well-designed but fairly simple mechanical aids. Costs would have been saved also.

Lifting techniques

Employees should be trained in at least basic requirements, especially: ensure that the route is clear beforehand; grasp the load firmly with palms, not fingertips; hold it close to the body; do not change grip; let the legs, not the back, take the strain; keep the spine straight; avoid jerking; never twist the body whilst picking up a load; lift in easy stages (e.g. floor to knee to start with); avoid overreaching.

Protective wear

This is often essential and its nature depends on the type of objects to be handled. Safety boots with protective toe-caps are an obvious example. Everyone has ten toes waiting to be squashed if they are not protected properly ... Hand protection, sometimes extending to the wrist or forearm, is necessary in handling goods with sharp edges. Gloves worn near moving machinery are generally dangerous as the machine may seize one quietly and drag in the hapless wearer to his considerable detriment. If in doubt about the correct protective wear, seek advice.

Manhandling objects thus has a sinister side, inflicting cruelties on the vulnerable human frame, especially the back. The time will come when the use of people for much of this work will be regarded as obsolete and indefensible as machinery takes over. This will also further productivity generally.

11

mechanical handling

What are the common hazards? • Overhead travelling cranes • Tower cranes • Mobile cranes • Construction hoists • Lifts • Garage hoists • Belt conveyors • Slinging

Loads of all sizes, shapes, weights and types – including live loads like human beings and animals – have to be lifted, carried and lowered by machinery.

Stories abound of cranes on North Sea oil platforms collapsing into the turbulent water with an expensive plop from time to time. On land, cranes and other lifting machines certainly do some remarkable things. Their favoured mishaps are overturning and dropping loads on whoever or whatever is beneath with a degree of irresponsible randomness or contacting high voltage over-head lines.

Of the reported accidents the majority are, in fact, caused by human failures.

What are the common hazards?

Most mechanical lifting machines have certain errant forms of behaviour in common and these require broadly similar precautions. The risk of overloading has to be countered by a range of measures including the marking of the maximum or safe working load for each piece of equipment.

There are British Standards and other standards for the manufacture and safe use of lifting equipment. All automatic indicators fitted to new cranes must comply with an HSE specification or offer an equivalent standard of performance. All machines must be well designed and soundly con-structed, be of good material and of adequate strength. Lifetime maintenance is essential. Periodic thorough examin-ation by a competent person such as an insurance company's engineer/surveyor is required. Records have to be kept. Nevertheless, different types of machines have characteristics

69

which call for special precautions. Only a few can be identified here.

Overhead travelling cranes

These versatile cranes have a wider variety of types of accident than any other as well as sharing the darker propensities of other machines. They can offer, for instance: electric shock; problems of access to the cab; limited visibility from the cab; possibility of knocking over nearby ladders and those who use them; mechanical hazards.

At the time of installation, key decisions have to be made which may be regretted later. For example, the maximum load of the crane and the height of the crane's installation above the floor are matters which cannot easily be changed later. Older cranes had ladder access to the cab but today raked stairways are needed.

A written procedure is needed for their operation and maintenance, and for work such as painting or cleaning which has to be done in close proximity to a crane. This requires a 'permit-to-work' system, e.g. attached to the statutory policy statement.

Crane drivers should be carefully selected; a sense of responsibility, good hearing and eyesight are all needed. They should be trained and competent for the job and formally authorised by you. You need to consider also having a second person available in case the regular driver is absent. A copy of the *HSE's Driver's Operating Card* which contains a checklist to be followed, should be given to each driver.

All lifting operations need to be planned by someone who is experienced. It is necessary, for example:

● to ensure that the crane's height and capacity are adequate for the load;
● to ensure that suitable lifting tackle is available;
● to select the best route for the load, avoiding persons and obstructions;
● to give responsibility for controlling the lifting operation to one person;
● to check that either the driver has an uninterrupted view

or provide a competent signaller to communicate with him.

Tower cranes

These monsters are common features of many a city's skyline. Particular problems arise when erecting and dismantling them. This work must be done in accordance with the manufacturer's recommendations. Any suggested deviation must first secure the manufacturer's approval.

If the manufacturer's handbook embodying the recommendations is a large volume it may be retained at the site office for reference. A short but accurate summary should then be provided for the use of those actually doing the work. Competent supervision at all stages is obviously needed. A sufficiently large clear area for stacking and handling the component parts will have to be provided.

A huge tower crane looming nearly 300 ft above a town centre street was lifting a six-ton jib from another crane which was being dismantled. But the lifting gear being used with it crumpled under the weight and slewed round out of control. One construction worker was injured while others leapt successfully out of the way. The falling jib just missed a crowded bus station.

Mobile cranes

The development of the modern massive mobile cranes has led to an increase in the number of accidents. Truck-mounted cranes have proved to be popular but they have limitations. The work they do is often carried out with outriggers and these must be extended to their correct position. Some do not have a slewing range of 360 degrees and this needs to be taken into account when positioning the crane. Like other cranes, they need firm level ground for lifting operations. There should be an assessment of the conditions by management beforehand, and good training and supervision should be arranged.

A mobile crane was entering a customer's yard from the towpath of a canal up a slight incline. Whilst being manoeuvred, it started to roll backwards slowly until it rested against a barge which was consequently pushed away from its moorings. This allowed the crane to subside gently into the water. The driver had the presence of mind to abandon his charge on the first sign of trouble.

Construction hoists

The use of a checklist is useful for maintenance purposes. Below is a suggested list which the HSE has drawn up for a maintenance procedure:

- hoistway enclosure
- landing gates
- cage or platform gates
- electrical and/or mechanical interlocks on gates
- cage or platform
- suspension devices for the cage or platform and counterweight (ropes, chains, racks and pinions)
- mast (including ties and locking bolts)
- travel limit switches
- guides
- guide shoes
- safety gear
- winches
- sheaves
- bearings
- counterweight
- electrical (cables, conduits, switches, etc.)
- buffers

Barrow or platform hoistways on building sites must be properly enclosed on all sides.

A council employee was visiting a site to deliver some building materials. He happened to walk into a partly-fenced platform hoist when the platform with its load of tiles fell and struck him. Though front gates were provided, the sides and rear of the hoistway were open.

Inclined hoists are increasingly used and they have an impressive repertoire of the undesirable things which can happen. The precautions are detailed and you should seek advice if you use them.

Lifts

Passenger and goods lifts inside buildings present problems for regular users and others, including members of the public. There are some basic safeguards such as interlocking devices on gates to prevent people falling down the lift shaft or being trapped between moving and stationary parts.

Lift maintenance requires careful planning and procedures and must be done by competent persons. This work involves bypassing the interlocks. It is essential to make certain that no one else can enter the lift as the gates may be open or can be opened even if the cage is not at the landing. A safe system of work is essential to keep people away and this should include substantial barriers and warning signs to supplement them.

The installation of a new lift was almost complete. The lift could be operated from the lift motor room in the basement, from the controls in the lift cage and by pressing the call buttons at any landing. The landing doors, although fitted, were not yet working automatically. A lift engineer who was thought to have been checking running clearances was killed as his head was trapped between the cage and the top of the basement landing. It is all too easy when concentrating on something to be off guard.

Garage hoists

Car vehicle hoists, as used in motor vehicle repair garages for working underneath cars, have had their own record of accidents.

A car was standing on a centre post vehicle hoist in a garage when the joint managing director was working under the vehicle with a mechanic. Suddenly the hoist crashed to the ground and fatally trapped the director. The investigation by HSE showed that the cause was lack of maintenance in conjunction with the bad practice of leaving the hoist in an elevated position for 48 hours over the weekend.

Belt conveyors

Widely used in moving goods and materials, conveyors of various kinds need to be assessed for safety. Among the special features is the need to provide access (e.g. bridges) from one side to another when long conveyors are in use. Otherwise people will climb over them which is dangerous even if the conveyor is stopped. The intakes of belts and pulleys are dangerous but accidents tend to happen particularly when someone tries to clear away material which is causing a jam. Maintenance personnel may be at risk if called upon to deal with adjacent machinery; or conversely, if dealing with a problem at a conveyor, they may be caught on nearby machinery.

A labourer received fatal injuries when he was trapped between the belt and tail pulley of a troughed belt conveyor powered by a 20hp motor. The belt was moving at 106 m (350 ft) per minute. What happened was that the labourer had reached between the belt and pulley with a shovel to remove some material from the pulley when the shovel and, as a consequence, his arm became trapped. The tail-pulley area was guarded only by a distance fence gate which was held in the shut position by a hand-tight bolt. A permit-to-work system was in fact operated at the conveyor but generally used only for removing blockages. The company was prosecuted and fined.

Slinging

Accidents due to poor slinging practice are a matter of continuing concern. Lack of training and inadequate supervision is blamed. Advice on an actual slinging and lifting sequence is as follows:

1. Know or find out the weight of the load.
2. Select the correct sling.
3. Fit the sling correctly, paying particular attention to the load's centre of gravity and the hitch of the sling.
4. Make a trial lift and during this and the actual lift keep people away from the area.

5. Set the load down in a clear area using bearers to support the load.
6. Release the sling carefully and beware of chain hooks snagging on the load.
7. After the lift, clear up the site and return the slings to their storage area.

12

work equipment

*Machine hazards • Abusing machines • 'Permit-to-work'
system • Precautions • Supervising employees*

Machines can be nasty, often biting the hand which feeds
them. They can be treacherous but usually require man's
cooperation in order to do their mischief. These tendencies
sometimes may be thwarted by good design but it is up to
you, the employer, to tame the machine and control the
employee. The same is true of other plant and equipment.

All work equipment has to be so constructed or adapted to
be suitable for the purpose for which it is used, from the
health and safety point of view. No more dangerous improvisation! The need will be revealed by the risk assessment. It
must be maintained in an efficient state, in efficient working
order and in good repair, maintenance being done by trained
personnel. Where there are other requirements in existence
(e.g. for lifts or scaffolding), they remain in force.

A 31-year-old driver was killed when his articulated dump truck
plunged 30m down the slope of a quarry excavation as a result
of a faulty braking system.

Duties are placed upon designers, manufacturers, importers
and suppliers but they do not relieve you, the employer and
user, from complying with current safety standards.

The heart of machine safety legislation, the long-established
requirement for the dangerous parts of machinery to be
securely fenced, has been ripped out by new legislation. It has
been transplanted to the new European-inspired regulations
which in fact say something similar but with embellishments.
From 1 January 1993 work equipment in general has had to
meet the requirements of the new regulations. The term 'work
equipment' is extremely widely drawn and includes machinery, appliances, apparatus and tools, for instance from a
ladder to a crane, or a drill bit to a tractor.

Certain categories of equipment such as machinery subject also to the Factories Act, which were in use before 1 January 1993 – the date on which the regulations for work equipment came into operation – have a concession. They need not comply fully with the new standards until 1 January l997. This delay is to enable employers to plan, budget and make all necessary arrangements to ensure the updating of standards as required by that date. It is not designed as a safety sabbatical.

Dangerous machinery and equipment must always be treated with constant respect.

First comes the widening of scope. Machinery is grouped with other plant to become a new class, work equipment.The new law applies to a staggeringly wide list of plant and other items, including machinery, all appliances, apparatus or tools and so on. Thus 'work equipment' includes items used in offices, schools, farms, hospitals, shops, leisure centres, residential care homes, laboratories and other places of work.

Machine hazards

That machinery can inflict serious injuries is well-known. In *Household Words* (1855) Dickens refers to a grouping of manufacturers as an 'association for the mangling of operatives'. Conditions are better today, but there is little room for complacency.

Machinery is non-discriminatory in its aggressive habits, and will attack anyone within reach: its operator, the maintenance personnel or anyone else. Fingers, hands and arms are preferred but other parts of the body are also drawn into its hurtful embrace. It amputates, cuts, fractures, crushes, lacerates and bruises whatever is allowed to come within its grasp. It has to be respected.

It is impossible to list all dangerous parts, but a useful guide is to consider the matter under the headings of: intakes between two moving parts; traps between a moving part and a fixed one; direct contact with a dangerous part; bits of machinery or material flying out.

Direct contact and other hazards

Some accidents happen from direct contact with an

inherently dangerous part such as revolving shaft, drill spindle or lathe stock bar. These are particularly treacherous because they look innocent, yet can wind into clothing or hair with a vice-like grip and cause grave injury. Direct contact with sharp-edged tools such as circular saws in woodworking, with set screws on revolving shafts, or with heated parts of plastic and other machines causes injury.

The operator of a chain-saw used in forestry work was re-starting the machine after a short break when, in a momentary lack of concentration, he caught the tip of the saw against the trunk of a small standing tree. This caused the chain-saw to kick back and lacerate his right side from the pelvic region to his armpit.

Something can even shoot out of a machine, as when a circular saw or vertical spindle moulder ejects its workpiece at a stunning velocity. Electrocution may result from contact with unearthed machinery. Machines have even been known to fall over and the modern cartridge tool has been shot in the wrong direction before today.

Among a machine's other tricks are overspeeding and, on occasion, ejecting parts of itself as when bits of a disintegrating abrasive wheel are hurled across a workshop.

Abusing machines

There are various ways of abusing machinery unintentionally, such as using the wrong machinery for a particular job.

In one case, a drilling-machine operator who was about to be made redundant, whiled away his time by polishing his own bowie knife on a buffing machine at work. He lost his balance and fell on the knife point. He was neither trained nor authorised to use this machine. The result was fatal.

The wrong machine may be used because the right one is not available; or because an employee misunderstands instructions, or is simply exercising misguided ingenuity. It is an abuse of machinery to use domestic types, such as food processors and washing machines, for industrial or commercial purposes.

A machine may be used in the wrong way, for example, by failing to clamp a workpiece, by misusing the safeguards provided, or it may be overloaded or overspeeded. Interfering with safeguards is regrettably not uncommon and may have disastrous consequences.

A fisherman was unloading fish from the hold of a fishing vessel by shovelling them into an elevator. While doing this, his foot was trapped between a down-running paddle and a fixed part of the elevator structure so that he was drawn into the machine. A second person tried to save him by pulling the safety switch but it failed to operate as it had been electrically bypassed previously by somebody unknown.

Another malpractice is to use a machine in an unsafe condition. Accidents may be caused, for instance, by faulty brakes or controls, loose parts, badly-maintained guards or interlocking devices, and rusted or worn parts. Power presses used in engineering are designed for use with metal but readily chop fingers if they are presented in the danger zone. These machines have to be regularly examined and tested according to specific regulations. The HSE has emphasised certain points such as:

- the person undertaking examinations must be fully competent
- defects in the machine as well as in the safety system have to be identified and promptly remedied
- the results must be recorded in a standard format
- matters requiring immediate attention should he highlighted in reports

---

A foreman was killed by the top rim of the casing of a hydro-extractor flying through the air when the corroded and overloaded basket ruptured during use. The machine had been bought second-hand some eight years before. The basket wall thickness should have been 8 mm but had corroded to a mere 2 mm. The employer did not know anything about routine inspections.

Cleaning plant and machinery

Cleaning plant and machinery leads to various kinds of abuse and maltreatment. A fundamental danger is that work equipment may be deliberately cleaned whilst it is in motion or it may be cleaned when put into motion by accident. The first is tempting because many machines are much easier to clean whilst they run. For instance, holding emery paper against a running shaft or spindle may look and feel innocuous but it is in fact a very dangerous practice.

Cleaning inside machinery which involves someone entering it presents hazards to the cleaner.

A 17-year-old factory worker went into a trough mixing machine to clean it with the machine stationary. Another employee, not knowing that there was someone inside the machine, switched it on in order to discharge some of the product. The youth was killed.

The official investigation revealed that the machine was only one month old and had been provided by the makers with the necessary interlocking system. The normal type of interlock for these machines ensures that they cannot be set in motion until the lid is securely closed and locked by a special device in the closed position. Also it ensures that the lid cannot be opened until the machine has come to rest. A 'permit-to-work' system may also be needed. In this case the interlocking device was found to be faulty. The employer was prosecuted and fined.

'Permit-to-work' system

For access to some machines a 'permit-to-work' system will have to be used in the same way as for access to confined space (see Chapter 8).

It is important to realise when a 'permit-to-work' system is called for, because sometimes this is not obvious until you give your mind to the matter. The underlying principle is that someone is required to do some work in a place which can be dangerous unless certain precautions are taken. The system has to be formalised in a written permission by an authorised person and addressed to a particular individual. This authorises entry to the place in question which is rendered safe for the duration of the work. Particular care is needed in planning the means of ensuring such temporary safe conditions. Although sometimes a 'permit-to-work' system is in operation, it may be faulty in some respect.

The lack of a satisfactory 'permit-to-work' procedure cost a machine fitter his life. He was crushed between the fixed and moving parts of a hydraulic hoist used for lifting skips of metal blanks. Work was being done on associated and integrated plant which was on an automatic cycle. The movement of this cycle was initiated when the fitter reached into the hoist enclosure and accidentally broke the infra-red beam. This caused the hoist to rise and he was trapped.

The official report pointed out that the plant had not been effectively isolated and a satisfactory 'permit-to-work' system had not been operated.

Precautions

Safeguarding is essential and wherever practicable (*not reasonably practicable*), fixed guarding must enclose the dangerous parts. This must therefore be done irrespective of cost. But when this is impossible, other guarding and, or protective devices are needed. A hierarchy of measures becomes evident:

1. Fixed enclosing guards.
2. Other guards or protective devices (e.g. interlocking guards).
3. Protection appliances (e.g. jigs or holding devices).
4. Special information, instruction, training and supervision.

All safeguards must be suitable for the purpose, of good construction and be properly maintained. They should not be easily bypassed or disabled; be at a sufficient distance from the danger zone; not unduly restrict the operator's view where this is necessary; designed to facilitate maintenance, preferably without having to interfere with the guarding or any protection devices.

Beware of apparently clever ideas like two-handed controls for they are often too easily circumvented by jamming a button down. 'Start' buttons and pedal controls should be shrouded to prevent accidental operation.

Sophisticated guarding of photoelectric type is acceptable in some cases but you will need specialist advice – and where programmable electronic systems are used.

Controls

There are requirements for controls, whether for starting, stopping, emergency or, for instance, the controlling of speed or temperature. Controls should be placed in suitable accessible positions, clearly visible and identifiable, being marked where appropriate. Electrical requirements for safety remain fully in force.

Plant controls are the 'man–machine' interface and their design and layout should comply with modern ergonomic standards. Ergonomics has been, at its simplest described as 'fitting the job to the worker', not vice versa. Yet many items of plant and equipment violate this principle. Workmen are seen reaching skywards to operate wheel controls, climbing over a forest of pipes to reach a control valve and otherwise performing acrobatic feats to operate plant.

Signs

Marking or warning signs are needed in some circumstances (e.g. the 'x-ray on' sign in a hospital physiotherapy department). New Regulations for signs have replaced the old ones and extended their scope to some extent. Where a risk cannot be eliminated or fully controlled, a safety sign is needed if it helps to reduce the risk. Signs are covered not only of the 'no smoking' type, but acoustic and hand signalling for instance. Firms which already comply with the relevant British Standard will need to make few changes, it is said.

A common misunderstanding is to believe that placing a warning sign in position is a substitute for making conditions as safe as possible. This is never so. But they are often useful to stress a point and, indeed, are sometimes essential as when it is necessary to remind people to wear hearing protection near noisy plants.

The display of information as part of a control system as on a computer monitor or an instrument's digital panel merits careful safety assessment. Is the right information being shown? Is it in the best form for the purpose? These and other questions should be asked when a risk assessment is carried out. Sometimes an excess of information may be displayed so that the operator has too much to assimilate and react to in the time available. After the nuclear accident in 1979 at Three Mile Island in USA, the subsequent OECD Report said: '... insufficient attention was being paid to the growing complexity of plant control rooms as more and more instrumentation was added at the request of design engineers or licensing authorities'.

Information and training

Employees are to be given adequate information about the hazards and precautions relating to their work with equipment of the various kinds. Supervisors and managers must also be well informed about such matters. Information must be easily comprehensible and include, for example, a warning of foreseeable abnormal situations with instructions as to the action to be taken.

This is in addition to any existing requirements (e.g. for users of woodworking machines). Young persons, especially, have to receive induction training and follow-up training with adequate supervision.

Comment

The remarkable characteristic of these new regulations is that they try to encompass all work equipment from a nail to a programmable electronic system. In view of the reputation of European Directives to lead to whimsical results at times, it is reassuring to realise that the HSE will enforce the legislation with its usual shrewd commonsense.

Supervising employees

Employees at any machine need to be trained and supervised. Every operator should know how to stop a machine even before he or she starts work at it. Young persons are prohibited from working at certain machines, and in other cases they can only be employed if they are either fully trained or are under proper instruction.

Care has to be taken when blockages in machines are

being cleared. All too often the machine gaily starts up, irrespective of where the person's hand is. The importance of safety during maintenance is underrated.

Loose clothing, dangling chains, finger rings, long hair and even straggly beards have tangled themselves with machinery and the machine always wins in such encounters. The precautions are obvious.

13

transport operations

*Road-type accidents at work • What are your
responsibilities? • Other hazards • Layout and
environment • The design of vehicles • Operation •
Specific types of vehicle • Dangerous goods*

Road-type accidents at work

Transport accidents happen on business premises as well as
on public roads, and usually with dire results. Many work
accidents occur when vehicles are reversing, being loaded,
unloaded or during maintenance and repair. They collide,
skid, overturn, burst into flame and run out of control.
There is one vital difference between road and work
accidents: a public authority provides, maintains and
controls public roads but not private ones. You – or your
landlord – do.

What are your responsibilities?

Many small firms have only a yard, or even a shared yard,
for the reception and despatch of goods, and some have
none. Some have complete road systems (e.g. caravan sites
and leisure parks). Whatever the size and nature of your
premises, you have responsibilities for traffic safety there.

You need to consider matters like the design, maintenance,
repair and use of all vehicles which you operate and the
safety of pedestrian movement within areas under your
control. The training and competence of your drivers are
matters for you. There are a number of special regulations
for certain dangerous loads which you carry and you need to
identify those which apply to your work. These are beyond
the scope of this book.

Other hazards

There is a risk of electrocution where vehicles with raised
parts, such as tipper lorries, come in contact with overhead

electricity transmission lines. In vehicle maintenance, work hazards are found in garage repair shops.

In one small factory a visiting sales director had his legs broken when the factory mechanic was changing a tyre without taking proper precautions. The locking rim flew out and struck him violently as no protective cage was used.

A major accident producer is the lift truck used indoors or outdoors. Employees going about their ordinary work are often unaware of the sudden danger from a truck which creeps up on them. Although lift trucks are by no means silent in operation, they are often used in noisy environments. When they push their way through swing rubber doors in a factory, for instance, they appear to arrive out of nowhere; that's why workpeople need to be particularly wary in such places.

The routes and operational areas for trucks need to be planned with safety as well as production in mind. For example, diesel-engined trucks (and other plant) should not be employed in places where there is a flammable atmosphere without special precautions. They also emit toxic gases and there must always be adequate ventilation where they are used.

Many, perhaps most, accidents are similar to road transport accidents but one difference is that workpeople may not be thinking about traffic as they go about their ordinary business.

The yard foreman at a container handling and repair depot walked into the side of an articulated trailer and tractor unit which was executing a tight turn and was run over by its rear wheels. The explanation was that he was concentrating on some papers he had in his hands.

At the heart of transport accidents at work, according to official reports, lie organisational defects, unsafe vehicles, faulty systems of work, inadequate training of drivers and a degree of ignorance and indifference by those involved, including managers.

Loading and unloading

Common accidents, especially with road vehicles, are: being run over by vehicles – often when reversing; injury when a vehicle overturns; being struck by a falling load; and falling from a height.

Access to elevated places is a long-standing problem in road vehicles (e.g. to the tops of loads in order to sheet them). Today some specialist vehicles carry their own apparatus for remote sheeting which can be done from ground level. Various other devices have been used but there remains a problem as employees have to clamber up and over loads for this or other reason, such as attaching slings to the load prior to unloading by crane. A ladder with suitable means of securing it in position, together with hand grips, may be the solution in some cases.

A lorry driver, while sheeting a load of pallets of empty plastic bottles, fell 4.25 metres from the lorry. The tops of the pallets were covered by a layer of cardboard giving a firm, level and non-slippery surface. He fell as he was pulling the first tarpaulin over the load.

Layout and environment

Vehicles often have to operate in places where there are blind corners, excessive gradients, inadequate turning room and poor lighting. The presence of pedestrians adds to the problems. Sometimes they cannot be easily seen but this is no excuse for running them down. It is up to you to assess the problem and deal with it before any accident happens, bearing in mind that members of the public might stray into workplaces.

At a disused airfield there were some small factories. Vehicles visiting them used to turn round at a large roundabout there. Neglect had caused blackberry bushes to spread into the roadway for about 1.2 m (4 ft), which should have put drivers on their guard. The driver of an articulated vehicle on the roundabout failed to notice a tramp in the bushes and drove into him.

The layout of any yard, road or road system should be safe. Is the entrance shared by vehicles and people, including customers and other visitors? Can you not separate them? A one-way system, if feasible, has much to commend it. Can you control the movement of people better? Any traffic and warning signs used have to conform to the Signs Regulations. Many sad tales can be told of accidents at loading bays and areas.

Reversing vehicles

Reversing vehicles contribute to deaths and injuries at work. There should be adequate turning room for vehicles or you should ensure that the driver reverses only with an assistant to guide him. Check too on the visibility conditions when it is dark.

At one retail store, articulated vehicles had to back up to a loading dock across a public car park. In spite of a risk of pedestrians (including children) being in the way, the drivers often reversed without an assistant. If the management had checked, they would have noticed that the otherwise excellent overhead lighting was obscured by the high vehicle which had to back up blindly to the dock in the dark.

Construction sites

On construction sites, especially where there are several subcontractors at work, traffic movements need to be well organised. The entrance and exit points should be planned as well as the places for depositing loads. Noise on building sites is such that men working there may not hear traffic approaching.

Road maintenance

This has been described as one of the most difficult areas of construction and transport safety because road works constitute a risk not only to the construction workers but to road users. Many serious accidents have occurred and it needs little imagination to envisage the result if a vehicle travelling at speed crashes into a road works site.

How best to prevent workers, materials and equipment from the site encroaching on to the carriageway being used by road traffic? Road signs constitute one means of control but the person in charge must know exactly how to set them out. The standards are described in a Department of Transport document, *The Traffic Signs Manual.*

Charging batteries

Charging batteries (e.g.for lift trucks) should be done in designated areas as this releases hydrogen which is liable to produce an explosive mixture in air.

In one case a battery had been taken off charge and was being fitted in a vehicle by a mechanic. His spanner, used to tighten the connections, slipped out of his hand and sparked off the oxygen-hydrogen mixture from the battery. An explosion shattered the battery case, pieces cut the man's face and he was splashed with acid.

The design of vehicles

Check whether a particular vehicle is designed for the carriage of passengers and, if not, enforce a ban. Sometimes a safety feature is necessary such as the roll-over bar for a tractor. Many dumpers still have starter handles with their built-in danger of kick-back whilst being turned. Their replacement by electrical starters would save many injuries.

Never modify a vehicle without the manufacturer's approval (e.g. fork extensions to fork-lift trucks). Some users have increased the counterweight with the intention of handling heavier loads without realising that this could lead to instability.

Good visibility for the driver is one of the most important needs as far as operational safety is concerned. The following factors, among others, should be considered: seating position of driver in relation to the layout of the vehicle and its superstructure or bodywork; devices to improve visibility such as Fresnel lenses and, for the rearward view, mirrors and radar or television units; wiping and washing facilities for windows and mirrors.

Poor standards of maintenance continue to be a significant factor in the cause of accidents. Routine maintenance is essential (e.g. checking the brakes frequently). Records should be kept of all maintenance work carried on and they should be legible and complete.

Operation

As road accident statistics show, careful driving is not second nature for the human race. As an employer you should select your drivers carefully, ensuring that they are competent to operate the vehicle they have to drive. On construction sites, for example, no one under the age of 18 is allowed to operate any vehicle. No one should operate any vehicle without express authorisation. Special regulations apply to road tankers and to the carriage of dangerous loads on the roads. These need to be consulted if they apply to your business.

Specific types of vehicle

Lift trucks cause many accidents and nearly half of them are officially classed as due to operator error. This emphasises the need for careful selection, training and supervision of operators. Lift trucks show no mercy to operators who maltreat them or even fail to park them safely.

A battery-operated fork-lift truck was used in a factory to move parts on pallets from one machine to another. Whilst waiting for a pallet to be loaded, the operator left the machine unattended. A pallet nearby, standing on its end, fell over when it was accidentally knocked, striking the long control-handle of the truck. This galvanised the truck into action and it struck the unsuspecting girl who was loading the pallet for the truck. The driver had failed to set the main switch off and there was no 'dead man's handle'.

Dumpers

As they chug round building sites, dumpers look easy to operate, especially the small ones. But any benign appearance is misleading as they will play high jinks, given half a chance. The dumper has a special ability for turning over and depositing its driver, itself and the load in an unceremonious manner wherever it chooses, whether reversing or not.

On one building site some bricklayers decided to take a dumper to save them time in their work. One of them, an untrained driver, loaded it with mortar and set off to the place where it was wanted. He travelled down a 1:8 gradient, apparently out of gear; the dumper gathered speed but the driver managed to steer it into a bank of earth. This threw him off and the dumper, true to its nature, decided to fall on top of him.

The dangers have become such that a special handy card has been published by the HSE to give to dumper drivers. It emphasises safe operation and advises them:

- to check the brakes before use
- to turn the starting handle properly to avoid injury
- to operate the machine carefully

This is a reminder and not a substitute for adequate training and supervision. You also have to ensure that the particular type of dumper is suitable for the work in hand, is properly used and well maintained. Records of maintenance should be kept, as with other vehicles.

Freight containers

Regulations spell out fuller requirements than can be summarised here and should be consulted. Some of the basic ones are that they must be of an approved type (and so marked), properly maintained and thoroughly examined periodically. Some of the essentials when they are used in harbour areas are: preplan the packing of goods in them to ensure compatibility of the contents with one another and to protect those who will have to unload them later; prevent overloading; check emptied ones before reuse to ensure that the previous load did no damage (e.g. by leaking corrosive substances which would affect the next load); take preventive action against the violent opening of doors once the doorlocks have been released. This can happen because of compression of the cargo or the use of air bags as dunnage between cargo and container walls. If pressurisation is suspected, the HSE recommends the placing of a lift truck against the doors to facilitate a more sedate opening.

Dangerous goods

The transport by road of dangerous substances in containers such as drums, bottles, carboys, cartons or skips as well as road tankers as such, is now subject to strict international-type regulations. They cover such matters as the design, construction and maintenance of the vehicles used; the provision by the consignor of information about the load; the carrying of that information by drivers; their adequate instruction, obligations on loading, unloading and stowage; the fitting of warning plates on vehicles; and supervision and safe parking of vehicles carrying larger quantities of dangerous substances or any amount of self-reacting substance.

There are details and strict rules for road tankers and tank containers used for the conveyance of dangerous substances by road.

Wherever dangerous substances are to be carried by road you should check the legal requirements with your trade association, HSE or other source of expertise.

14

display screen and other equipment

Display screen equipment • Pressurised systems • Electrical safety

There are too many types of plant to be discussed in a small book and the items chosen here are visual display units, pressurised systems and electrical installations. All are widely used and are now subject to regulations which may not be familiar to those who operate small firms.

Display screen equipment

Display screen equipment is subject to regulations which extend to a range of equipment defined as 'any alphanumeric or graphic display screen, regardless of the display process involved'. Common examples are the VDU (VDT) and microfiche. There are some exceptions such as display screen equipment in control cabs for machinery and portable systems provided that they are not in prolonged use.

The regulations apply to users (or operators in the case of the self-employed) but there are borderline cases which have to be considered. Anyone who uses such equipment more or less continuously will be a user. Where use is not continuous, other factors have to be considered which include the frequency, duration, intensity, demands on the person to produce accuracy which is critical and the amount of discretion the individual has over the extent and methods of use.

Word-processing pool workers, secretaries and typists using dedicated WP systems are obvious examples of users. Journalists and graphic designers may, for example, also be users under the regulations, according to circumstances.

Hazards

The object of the regulations is to protect individuals where necessary. There have been reports in the media of adverse health effects among VDU users (e.g. eye troubles, headaches, skin rashes, aching hands, arms and shoulders, stress and fatigue and even harm to unborn children of pregnant users).

The National Radiological Protection Board, the authority on the subject, is reported as saying that the radiation emitted is below acceptable levels and this remains the official view, but research is continuing. Any person worried about this should have the opportunity of discussing it with someone with up-to-date information on current authoritative scientific knowledge.

Assessment

Employers have to assess the risk to their own employees and others working at their workstations (e.g. 'temps'). It has to be systematic and involve the individuals concerned (after they have received training). One point to watch is that effects such as poor posture may not be the result of an unsuitable chair but because glare from the screen has caused the person to move in order to avoid it. The results should be recorded – including good features discovered. This may be done in writing or electronically. The assessment should be carried out by someone with the requisite knowledge (e.g. health and safety personnel), a specially trained line manager or outside expert help may be needed. The views of the employees and the safety representative, if any, should be taken into account.

Reducing risks

Action should be taken straight away to deal with the risks identified. This may be a matter of repositioning furniture or providing a more suitable chair; adjusting the position of the screen; fitting blinds to eliminate glare or correcting the lighting. In setting out the workplace, the requirements of good ergonomic practice should be observed.

For reported stress or fatigue, any obvious defects will need to be remedied. One way may be to give the individual more control of his or her work rather than having to be paced by the equipment (which is akin to the undesirable and stressful practice of being paced by a machine in industry). Training is imperative and this includes mode of operation and use of software as well as health and safety. The use of ergonomic principles is important.

Pressurised systems

The regulations are designed to protect people at work from the risks posed by uncontrolled releases of stored energy from pressure systems. They apply to all places of work.

Types of plant

The range of plant covered is wide and has special relevance not only to industry but also to non-industrial premises. Familiar examples are steam boilers, compressed-air systems (including air receivers and associated pipework) and large refrigeration systems as used in commerce and the retail trades. Small steam plant, for example, is found in many catering establishments.

Application

Regulations impose safety requirements for the construction, installation, repair, modification and use of pressure systems and transportable gas containers at work. The intention is that all parts of pressurised plant (including the interconnecting pipework and fittings, protective devices and control equipment) should be regarded as a single pressure system. This is necessary because safety is critically dependent upon the integrity of the whole system. 'The chain is as strong as its weakest link'.

Detailed requirements

The regulations set out the broad objectives, leaving the details to be dealt with in *Approved Codes of Practice* issued by the HSE together with *Guidance Notes* published to supplement them. If you have pressurised plant you will need to obtain the relevant Codes of Practice.

Written scheme

A characteristic of the new arrangements is that, if you have the plant in question, you will have to draw up a written scheme setting out the details of necessary examinations of plant and the intervals between them. The pressure systems code sets out in detail how you should go about deciding the scope of the scheme as it applies to you. For this, you will need the advice of a competent person and the code sets out acceptable criteria for persons certifying and drawing up such schemes.

Gas cylinders

One approved code deals with gas cylinders of which there are an estimated 30 million in this country. They are all miniature pressure vessels and some operate at very high pressure.

The code sets out in detail how cylinders should be stored and handled to reduce risks. Also it includes the precautions necessary at filling plants to ensure that only cylinders fit for further service are refilled. See *Safe Pressure Systems* (HSE).

Electrical safety

Electricity does not just mean a shower of sparks if it goes wrong, the HSE points out. Shock, burns, flame and explosion can result from taking unnecessary risks. Cable strikes can mean misery for thousands of people as workers digging on building sites hit underground electricity cable-often at personal risk.

The modern regulations apply to all employers, self-employed and employees. Work on such places as research establishments, schools, farms, and domestic premises are all now under this protective umbrella. Industrial establishments will of course be covered but to a higher standard than before. The regulations set out basic electrical safety principles as opposed to detailed requirements. Good practice must always be followed. One point which is greatly emphasised is to switch off first before working on electrical equipment. Two Approved Codes of Practice accompany the regulations. Reference should also be made to current regulations of the Institution of Electrical Engineers.

Two points to emphasise for small firms are, firstly, only those who are electrically qualified should deal with electrical faults and installations. Secondly, electrical installations should be periodically checked for safety by qualified personnel. For electricians there are rules for protection especially where live working is unavoidable.

15

safety management

Safety as part of management • Policy • Risk assessment • Accident prevention • Construction management • Conclusion

Safety as part of management

The significance of health and safety at work from the viewpoint of any undertaking, large or small, is that it is part of the function of managing. Safety – which here, as elsewhere in this book, includes health – is not an optional extra to be added when funds are ample and time is available. It is required right now: it is an inherent strand in the cloth of management.

When you plan and organise your business, draw up your budget, recruit and train staff, give orders and monitor the work being done, the safety implications are part of the decision-making process. If you sell or hire out products, you similarly must consider safety together with other relevant matters. The Certificate of Insurance for Employer's Liability must be displayed in your premises.

Each employee of a small firm should not be at greater personal risk than if employed by a large firm. If you lose your hand in a machine, it is the same personal disaster whether it happened in a small or a large concern.

It is facile to 'explain' an accident away by simply saying 'the man was careless' or 'the management was at fault'. Both are often true but this 'explanation' conceals more than it reveals. An inadvertent slip by an employee, a momentary lapse perhaps, may have been triggered by tiredness after a long spell without a break, or by inadequate training, or by lax supervision which allowed an undesirable habit to develop, or by pressure and stress, or any combination of these factors.

Work-related stress is seen today as a major contributor to sickness absence, and small firms can be badly affected by the absence of a key employee at any level. Managers and supervisors are affected by stress as well as other employees. A number of other factors have to be considered when examining stress at work but only a few can be stated here, such as excessive periods of repetitive or monotonous work; uncertainty about what exactly is required; fear for his or her job; interpersonal conflict; or an over-demanding work schedule, are common ones.

You who are in charge generally control the environment in which all your employees will work and obviously this must be acceptable. You mastermind their conditions of work even though you may consult your workforce, which can be helpful. But all this brings responsibility. The responsibility of deciding not only the quality of working life your workforce shall have, but also the impact your business will have upon the local community (e.g. pollution).

Policy

You have a safety policy, however vague, simply by your intentions expressed in action – or inaction. Is your policy towards employees, customers and the public generally what it ought to be? Some specific decisions have to be made. For instance, do you intend to employ young persons? If so, are you prepared for the extra training these inexperienced youths must have? You may decide to employ persons over retirement age, part-timers, married women 'returners', non-smokers or some other particular group. You make decisions of many kinds but must heed the safety implications.

The employer is ultimately liable for what goes on in his organisation. Safety is woven into the management functions and is not an add-on.

Statutory policy statement

As part of the planning function, the employer has to prepare a written policy statement. To help small firms, the HSE has published a useful booklet which you just fill in as appropriate. It is entitled *Writing Your Health and Safety Policy Statement.* This is set out in three parts.

Section A: General statement of policy. This makes a general declaration based on your obligations under the legislation and states who is responsible for what.

Section B sets out the general arrangements regarding such matters as fire safety, first aid and the reporting of accidents. *Section C* deals with the hazards in your undertaking together with the safety rules you have drawn up to deal with them.

The document is signed by you and kept available at all times. Its contents have to be brought to the attention of all employees (e.g. by issuing a personal copy or posting up on a notice board permanently). It has to be kept up-to-date as changes arise. Only firms employing five or fewer persons are exempt. Although intended for employees, increasingly outsiders are asking to see a copy (e.g. customers on whose premises your employees work). Similarly, you may wish to see the policy statement of firms with whom you are collaborating (e.g. in construction work).

Risk assessment

These two buzz words in essence refer to a safety check carried out by a competent person (probably the senior executive if knowledgeable enough). First, it identifies the health and safety hazards in your firm, including off-site ones if your employees work away from base.

A hazard is anything which can cause harm (e.g. a dangerous substance) and risk is the chance of harm actually being done. Risk assessments should identify the significant hazards arising out of work of all kinds, evaluating their extent and taking into account whatever precautions are already being taken. The severity of potential harm has to be included as risk reflects both the likelihood of harm resulting and its severity. The result of such an assessment points the way to additional safeguards which are required. Clearly, all 'rules and regulations' have to be observed in all work activities. Where five or more persons are employed, the results of risk assessments have to be recorded and the records kept.

There is a vast amount of knowledge about hazards and the precautions to be taken – which by their nature aim to reduce or even exclude the risk (e.g. by substituting a safe substance). This book should help you to identify both hazards and necessary precautions. If you employ five or more people, you have to write down your findings and keep the results for inspection. Updating is required when necessary.

Information

Your employees should be informed of the hazards of their work and the precautions to be taken, which you need to enforce through the management chain. Sometimes outsiders are exposed (e.g. contractors working in your premises may be unaware that you are using flammable materials). They should be informed about this so that they will take necessary precautions. Linked with information is training.

Training

All recruits need some induction training both for their particular work and in general (e.g. the fire precautions). Training may be on-the-job or off-the-job (e.g. in the local technical college) according to need. Other employees also need training both for their ordinary work and when transferred to other work. For some dangerous machines such as circular saws special training is required incorporating the safety aspects. Refresher training is often needed from time to time.

Construction management

Special legislation lays down requirements for those in the construction industry by new regulations. Not only builders but others such as architects now have statutory duties for safety.

Key features include the setting up of a team for each project including the client, the designer, the planning supervisor, the principal contractor and other contractors. The self-employed are included. Employees too have a voice in safety matters. Teamwork is essential.

The client chooses a planning supervisor and principal contractor who are competent and have adequate resources for the safety requirements. The client may appoint himself to either of these positions or both.

The designer (i.e. anyone carrying on an undertaking for the preparation of the design) must design out all risks as far

101

as possible and provide information about significant risks not known to the others. Adequate attention must be paid to future risks (e.g. cleaning).

The planning supervisor sets out a health and safety plan and starts a health and safety file. He has to ensure as far as is reasonably practicable that the design of the structure complies with safety requirements.

The principal contractor develops the health and safety plan, co-ordinates the activities of all contractors to ensure safety and checks that all employees are properly trained and given the necessary information. He has to ensure co-operation between contractors, complete the health and safety plan and provide safety information to contractors. All contractors and the self-employed have to co-operate with the principal contractor.

The health and safety plan

This has to be prepared before the work starts. It brings together information for the client, designer and principal supervisor to assist the principal contractor in the preparations. The plan is developed throughout the construction phase with details of arrangements for monitoring so as to exclude risks. The health and safety file is like a maintenance manual, stating health and safety information for each structure.

Notification

The notification of the project has to be sent to the HSE (which enforces the regulations), giving certain particulars before work starts. The planning supervisor has to ensure this is done.

Accident prevention

In planning your activities, consider what is meant by 'safety' in any particular context. There is misunderstanding, for instance, about the difference between accident prevention and safety. Accident prevention means what it says. Safety is a wider term and embraces accident prevention and damage limitation, that is dealing with the consequences of accidents if they do occur. A guard for a machine is an accident-prevention measure but first aid is a damage-limitation one. The exclusion of sources of ignition from the workplace is an example of accident prevention but fire extinguishers are classed under the heading of damage limitation.

The basic safety rule is that you need both to prevent accidents as far as possible and to deal with the consequences if an accident does happen. This may seem obvious but it is often overlooked.

Conclusion

The underlying philosophy of the health and safety legislation today is that of self-regulation. As an employer you have to consider health and safety in your decision-making. This book aims to help you in this. But you will need to keep yourself informed and up-to-date. Things are constantly changing and, to give one example, robotics will be more common in small firms one day. Perhaps in yours.

You set standards and it is the discipline you enforce which is so important in ensuring safety. Your decisions directly affect the quality of working life as far as your employees are concerned.

16

your employees' rights and duties

*Appointment • Young persons • Pregnancy and work •
Training • Information • Enforcing company rules •
Trade unions*

All employees are entitled to safe conditions at work. They
also have a duty to take reasonable care of themselves at
work and of others who may be affected by the way in which
they do their work.

Scattered through many regulations are duties placed
upon employees e.g. to use the safeguards provided and not
to interfere with things provided for the health and safety of
others.

Appointment

There are few restrictions when appointing people. Obviously a heavy goods vehicle driver needs the appropriate licence; others, such as those who mount any kind of
abrasive wheels, must have the statutory training before they
undertake such work for you.

Disabled persons have the same rights as the able-bodied.

Young persons

These are males and females over compulsory school age but
under 18 years of age. They will need careful – and perhaps
repeated – instruction on basic safety requirements. Make
clear to them what they must not do (e.g. operate certain
machines). Arrange for them to be supervised closely,
particularly at first.

Certain dangerous machines such as dough mixers, meat
mincers and the office guillotine, even if hand-operated, have
special rules. No young person is allowed to work at any

specified machine unless he or she has been fully instructed about its dangers and the relevant precautions. Then they must have either been sufficiently trained to work at any of the listed machines or be under the adequate supervision of someone with thorough knowledge and experience of the particular machine.

Pregnancy and work

New regulations apply to three groups of workers: pregnant women, those who have recently given birth and those who are breastfeeding. Employers have to assess the safety of these groups in the course of risk assessment. If a risk remains which the employer cannot eliminate, it will be necessary to change their working hours or conditions of work or offer them alternative work. If all else fails they should be given paid leave for as long as necessary.

Possible hazards at the workplace include lifting and handling tasks, harmful substances, radiations and certain chemical and biological agents.

Training

Everybody needs training in health and safety. This may be 'on the job', i.e. at work, or 'off-the-job', for example at the local technical college. Health and safety should be taught as an integral part of the job. The hazards of the work and of the working environment must be brought to the attention of employees who have to be informed about the risks and precautions of their work.

A sufficient number of employees should be trained in the use of fire extinguishers of the type you provide. Someone – preferably more than one person – should be trained in first aid.

Information

Allied to training is the giving of information, both verbal and written. An official poster *Health and Safety Law* has to be displayed at the place of work or issued as a leaflet to all employees. Some pocket-size leaflets and cards are issued by HSE for the information of employees.

Examples from many are:

- *Save Your Breath. Campaign against occupational lung disease – advice for employees.*
- *Save Your Skin. Occupational contact dermatitis.*
- *Beware of Noise.*
- *Safe Working with Small Dumpers.*

If you do not recognise any trade union in your business, you may still have safety representatives from the work force. They may, for instance, be elected by the employees and you may well find them useful allies in promoting safety at work.

Proposals for compulsory consultation with employees by employers are currently under discussion. At the present time, those firms, large or small, which recognise trade unions have to give consultation and associated rights to employees nominated by the unions as safety representatives. The intention now is to extend rights to employees of firms which do not recognise trade unions. It is suggested that the work force may elect their own representatives or the employer may consult employees directly. Until the official discussions with business are concluded, the precise details will not be known, but it is certain that consultation rights will be extended.

Enforcing company rules

Every firm has some health and safety rules which should be clear. Make sure that everyone knows and obeys the rules, and do not rely merely on notices. Some rules (e.g. against violence at work) are implied.

Disciplinary procedures

What happens when someone breaks the safety rules? For a minor breach a verbal reprimand may suffice but you may have to invoke the formal disciplinary procedure as for other forms of wrong behaviour, i.e. the sequence of (1) oral warning; (2) written warning; (3) final written warning, pointing out possible dismissal; (4) dismissal or suspension. Instant dismissal may sometimes be justified but you need to be very sure of your ground and act fairly.

In this case the failure was so serious a matter that no prior warnings were needed before dismissal. It is more usual to invoke the formal procedure but it is important always to allow the employee to explain his or her behaviour. Also rules must never be enforced in an arbitrary manner such as against one employee but not another in similar circumstances.

Constructive dismissal

The boot may be on the other foot if you as employer fail to play your part in safety. If you fail to provide something necessary for health and safety, the employee may resign and claim that he was forced to do so in effect because of your failure. This is known as *constructive dismissal*, and you would be financially liable for it.

Payment system

If you pay employees by some kind of incentive system, you will need to ensure that this does not encourage them to cut corners in safety. Workers have been known to remove machine guards, for instance, in order to speed up output and earn more money. The answer usually lies in a safe system of work, discipline and supervision.

Trade unions

If you recognise a registered trade union, it may appoint safety representatives from among your employees. If so, it has to notify you in writing. Safety representatives have many functions, such as carrying out safety inspections, investigating accidents, representing the interests of the employees in matters concerning their health, safety and welfare at work, and to secure information from inspectors.

They are allowed time off with pay to do this and for attending certain training courses. They are expected to keep up-to-date with the health and safety requirements relating to the workplace.

17

maintenance work

Means of access and place of work • Work equipment •
Welding • Planned plant maintenance • Wear and tear •
Hand tools

Maintenance work includes a wide range of activities, often in places difficult to reach such as a valve within a jungle of pipes. It would be a good idea if maintenance personnel came from a long line of acrobats at some establishments. Maintenance includes the repair, servicing, restoration, lubrication, cleaning of all types of plant, machinery, vehicles, structures and much else. There are opportunities for injury, such as: being caught up in an ungrateful machine after clearing a blockage without proper precautions; falling off ladders; toppling off roofs; dropping through fragile roofs; crashing through skylights; being trapped in lifts; being overcome by fumes or gases; being cut (e.g. on a saw) or being bruised by a faulty hammer.

If all else fails to maim, there is the chance of health problems from handling asbestos used, perhaps, as insulation material.

You have to accept prime responsibility and need to check on the type of work which has to be done under your control. Certain common hazards may be singled out for further consideration: means of access and places of work; mechanical hazards; welding. Do not overlook maintenance work when carrying out risk assessment.

Means of access and place of work

A ladder may be the means of access or the place of work itself. It should be suitable for the job in hand (e.g. not too short) and should be properly secured (e.g. by lashing). (See also Chapter 4.)

The place of work for maintenance may be just about anywhere: in, on or under plant, machinery, vehicles, buildings and so on. Review the places where such work has to be done, however infrequently, and you may find some awkward spots for access. So try to improve matters by altering the layout and other relevant features.

Buildings

The maintenance of buildings often takes place for periods of short duration so that there is a tendency not to bother with scaffolding or other access equipment at each job. The best solution may be to provide permanent walkways to give access (e.g. on roofs). In cases where a safety belt or harness provides the only effective means of protection, built-in permanent anchorages may be the answer (e.g. for window cleaners).

Another feature which affects the way the work is done is that the maintenance is necessary precisely because the building has deteriorated. This is especially important when access to a roof is required. Roofing material, non-fragile when installed, may deteriorate in time and, whilst externally looking no different, it may be lethal to step on. Fragile panels in a roof may be indistinguishable from the rest of the roof through painting, weathering, or the deposit of dirt or dust. Asbestos roofs are fragile and should not be stepped on directly.

Two brothers were sent on to a roof to clean the roof lights which had been painted, like the roof itself, with bituminous paint. The first brother, not identifying the roof lights, fell through one but fortunately landed astride a metal stanchion in the factory. He then proceeded to climb back on to the roof to warn his brother of the danger but was too late. His brother had fallen to his death through another roof light.

There may be difficulties in carrying out maintenance in buildings such as blocks of flats, where there are residents. Scaffolders may not be able to use the windows for through ties – and, of course, the residents will need protection, e.g. from falling objects. In addition, it is more than usually necessary to take precautions against children scrambling up the scaffolding or otherwise getting into danger.

There are special precautions to be taken when someone has to enter a confined space where there is a risk of being overcome by gases or fumes or oxygen deficiency.

The precautions centre on what is known as a 'permit-to-work system' which is discussed in Chapter 8.

Work equipment

Risks associated with work equipment are discussed in Chapter 12 and of these a number arise in maintenance work and in general similar precautions have to be taken.

As far as possible, machines and other work equipment should be so constructed to enable any maintenance work to be done without risk. If, for instance, the work cannot be done with the machine or plant stationary, it is necessary to adopt safeguards to protect the maintenance personnel (e.g. by temporary guarding). There is no exemption for maintenance personnel from health and safety protection.

Welding

Between them, electric arc and gas welding present a medley of problems: damage to the eyes; burns to the skin; electric shock; fume and gas inhalation; fire; explosion.

Not only are the welder's eyes exposed to the electric arc, those of persons nearby are too. The welder's skin is also at risk. Electric shock is another possibility to be taken seriously. Fumes and gases may be produced by the process itself, either from the metal being welded or the electrodes being used. Sparks given off are quite good at setting things on fire and a sudden explosion can be staged by trying to weld an 'empty' tank which has contained flammable liquids. Even when apparently empty, a tank may contain a residue of flammables. Careful preparatory procedures are needed.

In one factory a workman had to remove the tops of some drums which had contained petrol. Relying on his nose – a quick sniff indicated all as clear – the man applied the welding torch to the drum. A muffled explosion resulted, his clothing started to burn and the drum and contents flew some distance to become flaming piles on the floor. No precautions had been taken and it was found that heavier petroleum fractions had been secreted in the drum's seams, ready to explode on the application of heat.

Precautions

Protective goggles and face screens where appropriate, suitable gloves and apron protect the welder. Personal protective equipment should be of approved type. Screening off the welding area is needed to protect outsiders from 'eye-flash' injury which can happen as the result of one glance at the arc. Electricity safeguards according to statutory standard are always essential. Fumes and gases may often be removed by good natural ventilation but sometimes mechanical extraction is required.

It is imperative that employees receive proper training and instruction and, as necessary, supervision. Knowledge of the dangers does not come naturally.

A youth was cutting through an oil-filled pipe. As his cutting torch cut through the last portion of the metal, the hot oil squirted out and ignited, burning his face and setting his clothes on fire. He was badly burned and permanently disfigured.

Planned plant maintenance

Some items of plant like lifts have to have regular statutory examination and maintenance but all plant and machinery need it. Some of the main benefits from a planned system of maintenance are: work injuries on faulty machines are reduced; plant availability is increased; production is less likely to be suddenly interrupted; the standard of maintenance is higher; better use of labour force is facilitated because of reduced breakdowns; machinery and plant last longer; machinery and plant maintain their value better.

Those who undertake maintenance and associated examination and inspection duties have their own hazards to face and it is easy to become complacent about them.

A passenger lift was being installed in a commercial building under construction and had almost been completed. A lift engineer entered the pit without isolating a second lift and was struck by the balance weight of the neighbouring lift.

It is essential that anyone who is working in a lift shaft shall be protected from contact with adjacent lifts which are still in operation. A safe procedure should be drawn up, taught and always followed.

Wear and tear

Every item of work equipment, including safety devices, is subject to wear and tear; deterioration in performance may be insidious and undetected. Only regular checking and maintenance can keep machinery in tip-top condition.

In making adjustments to machines, it is often overlooked that there is no exemption for maintenance personnel; they must use safeguards even when trying out the machine afterwards. Records of adequate details must be kept for some plant and machinery under specific legislation. You have a duty to maintain plant and machines in good and safe condition. For your own purposes as well as to satisfy the professional interest of inspectors, you should keep systematic records. When a particular register is required according to regulations (e.g. for power presses), it should be used.

Hand tools

These, too, must obviously be properly maintained in the interests of the work as well as of safety. Points which particularly need to be borne in mind for commonly used tools are: hammers – avoid split, broken or loose shafts and worn or chipped heads; heads must be properly secured to the shaft; files should always have a proper handle in good condition; chisels – the cutting edge should be kept sharpened to the correct angle; and steps taken to prevent mushroom heads; screwdrivers must never be used as chisels, and hammers should never be used on them – avoid split handles; spanners – avoid splayed jaws and scrap any which show signs of splaying. Keep a sufficient range of sizes to prevent improvising.

18

enforcement and the cost of failure to comply

To whom is a duty owed? • The HSE • Local authority inspectors • Powers • Issue of notices • Prosecution • Penalties • Manslaughter • Civil liability

Health and safety legislation is part of the criminal law. As an employer, manufacturer, designer, supplier, importer, occupier, etc. you may have duties. As an individual you have, too.

To whom is a duty owed?

The safety of people such as customers as well as employees is covered by this legislation. Penalties can be severe for contraventions. In addition, you owe a common law duty to employees and others for whom you should provide reasonably safe conditions.

The HSE

These letters stand for Health and Safety Executive. Although the underlying philosophy in health and safety is one of self-regulation, in practice a fairly elaborate system of enforcement is necessary. There are two kinds of inspectorates: those of central government and those of local authorities.

Fire authorities have important specialist duties but are not part of the HSE. The HSE itself acts as agent for the Ministry of Agriculture, Fisheries and Food, under the Food and Environment Protection legislation. There is also collaboration with various government departments on matters of joint interest.

Organisation

In addition to the headquarters organisation, the HSE has 20 geographic areas, each with a specialist National Industry Group (NIG) centred on it. (See Appendix.)

Local authority inspectors

Whilst HSE inspectors generally deal with manufacturing and major or complex types of workplaces, local authorities are particularly involved with offices, wholesale and retail distribution and service industries such as hotels and catering. Many small firms will be subject to inspection by local authorities. The nominated inspectors are usually Environmental Health Officers (EHOs). Liaison is maintained with the HSE as the 'lead' authority on health and safety.

Powers

All inspectors have the same powers under the law:

1. To enter your premises at almost any time.
2. To inspect them.
3. To investigate accidents.
4. To take photographs, recordings and measurements.
5. To examine relevant documents.
6. To take samples.
7. To order the dismantling of dangerous articles.
8. To take away articles and substances.
9. To question anyone on the premises.
10. To require them to sign a written declaration.
11. To require facilities and assistance for carrying out their duties.
12. To issue Prohibition Notices and Improvement Notices.
13. To prosecute.

Inspection policy

In spite of this formidable list, it is official policy to promote compliance with good standards, to advise rather than prosecute. Inspectors are ready to discuss your problems although lack of funds does not excuse you from providing safe conditions. The HSE issue safety leaflets for employers, employees and others to give information and advice.

Issue of notices

Inspectors can issue two kinds of written notice, both 'on the spot': Improvement Notices; Prohibition Notices. They can be addressed to any person, individual or corporate, but most are issued to employers.

In one case, so an anecdote says, an inspector issued a Prohibition Notice to an employee, forbidding him to move his car in the company car park. It was, in the inspector's opinion, too dangerous to use on the premises.

Although no prior warning is needed before issuing either kind of notice, an inspector will discuss the matter and any problems you may have, before issuing it. Both kinds are legal documents and are to be taken seriously.

Improvement Notices

These notices require the employer (or other person addressed) to make specified improvements by a certain date which will be more than 21 days hence. This period is allowed for you to appeal to an industrial tribunal if you so wish. Few appeal and of those who do, few succeed.

If, for instance, you are required to fit a certain safeguard within three months but the supplier informs you that he cannot supply within that period, tell the inspector and seek an extension of the time. But do not wait until the three months have elapsed before doing so, for the inspector is unlikely to be able to help you then. Failure to comply with such a notice (which is based on an alleged breach of the law) may land you in court.

Prohibition Notices

These are even more severe documents. An inspector may issue one whenever he or she considers that there is a risk of serious personal injury or health risk. Some notices take effect immediately but some are 'deferred'. The former may order you to cease an operation immediately and you must comply.

Failure to comply with such notices is one of the most serious offences under the legislation, so do what it says. You must expect the inspector to come back to check compliance with the notice.

A director of three construction companies was sentenced to 18 months' imprisonment, suspended for two years, after one of the companies had been involved in asbestos removal without a statutory asbestos licence and in contravention of a Prohibition Notice. He was also fined £1,200 for various other offences. The fines would have been higher, said the Judge, but he had been convinced that the director was devoid of assets.

You have a right to appeal within 21 days but, unlike the Improvement Notice, you must comply immediately.

Some key differences

Improvement Notice	*Prohibition Notice*
Orders a specified improvement	Bans something
Requires this by a certain date	Generally operative immediately
Need not comply for 21 days or more	Does not allow this delay
Breach is a summary offence	Breach is an indictable offence

Prosecution

Although inspectors prefer to secure compliance without prosecuting, they will sometimes be compelled to take legal action, for instance, if:

1. A serious offence has been revealed by an accident.
2. You have persistently contravened the legislation.
3. You have failed to comply with a notice.

Legal proceedings are usually taken in the magistrates' court (in England and Wales) but more serious indictable offences may be taken in the crown court. The inspector who proposes to prosecute submits a report, with supporting evidence, to higher authority for approval. In Scotland, this report submitted to the Procurator Fiscal who decides whether to proceed.

Any person, individual or corporate, may be prosecuted. In most cases it is the employer who is prosecuted but there are exceptions.

Two employees in a furniture factory were fooling around. One, a man of 56, threw a hammer at the head of the other, a 17-year-old youth. The teenager threw a cartridge of staples at the older man. Neither intended to injure the other as it was just horseplay. But the inspector prosecuted both – successfully – for failing to take reasonable care for another person at work.

Penalties

The maximum fine in a magistrates' court is currently £5,000 on each count. In the crown court, fines are unlimited and for the more serious offences, such as failing to comply with a Prohibition Notice, up to two years' imprisonment may be imposed. Costs may also be awarded. Appeals are possible to the general legal system but you will need the necessary funds!

The first immediate custodial sentence passed under the health and safety legislation took place in January 1996. An employer was sentenced to three months' imprisonment for five breaches of the regulations applying to asbestos. He was also ordered to pay £4,000 costs. A factory was being demolished with an excavator without any precautions being taken to prevent the spread of asbestos in roofing sheets and in pipework lagging. The HSE prosecuted him and this was the result.

Manslaughter

The first manslaughter case (as far as is known) in connection with health and safety legislation was on 1 December 1989 when a one-year prison sentence, suspended for two years, was imposed on a company director. The case arose from an accident at the workplace.

117

At the company's factory, an employee was killed in a plastics crumbling machine. Both the HSE and the police investigated the matter. Two of the directors (brothers) were prosecuted for unlawful killing and various other offences. One director was found guilty of manslaughter and both of various other offences. Fines totalling £47,000 were also imposed as well as the suspended prison sentence.

Civil liability

In addition to duties owed under the criminal safety legislation there is a civil liability placed upon employers for the safety of their employees, visitors and others affected by what they do. This is not limited to matters which are in breach of the safety legislation, although they are included.

It centres on negligence which in ordinary language means failing to do what you should do or doing what you ought not to do with the consequence that someone is injured. That person may claim damages from you (i.e. monetary compensation). In practice, your insurance company will play the leading role in the negotiations which result.

A lady staying at caravan site slipped in the shower in the baths block and was injured. She fell and was temporarily unconscious and it was a little time before she could summon help as there was no one around. In due course she claimed against the owner-occupiers of the site. The investigation – a private one as the claim was a civil one – revealed a fault in the design of the base of the shower which caused it to be slippery in use. The case was settled out of court.

When an accident occurs on your premises and someone is injured a civil claim may be made by the injured person. If it is a notifiable one, an inspector from the HSE or local authority, as the case may be, may investigate it. But this is separate from the civil claim which will first come to your notice when you receive a letter from the victim's solicitors. You should notify your insurance company immediately and they will then look into the matter and carry it forward.

You may expect a visit from the solicitors or their representative(s) acting for the injured person. They will investigate the accident on your site where it happened. If the claim goes forward it may be settled out of court by your insurance company in negotiation with the victim's solicitors or it may go to a civil hearing in court. In the latter case, you may have to be present personally and one or more of your employees may have to attend court also. Needless to say, this costs time and hence money, even though the insurance company will pay any award made. As well as the cost, the interruptions to your work and perhaps some worry about it all, you must expect to have additional paperwork to deal with.

19

essential documents, reports and notices

Information, advice and warning • Licences and certificates • Records of statutory examination • Health records • Notification • Posters and notices

It is inevitable that there should be many documents associated with health and safety at work. They may be broadly classified under the following headings:

1. Information, advice and warning.
2. Licences and certificates.
3. Records of plant examination.
4. Health records.
5. Notification.

Information, advice and warning

Various notices must be posted up at the workplace. These include: a copy of safety regulations applying to the premises (e.g. Woodworking Machines Regulations); at all places of work, a notice entitled *'Health and Safety Law'. What You Should Know* should be posted up or, alternatively, a leaflet copy should be given to every employee. If you opt for this alternative, do not forget to give a copy to every new recruit.

Reference documents aimed at employers include a series of detailed technical documents known as *Guidance Notes*. Codes of practice associated with regulations are also available as well as short leaflets offering practical advice in potted form. These include *Health and Safety in Small Clothing Factories* and *Review Your Occupational Health Needs. Employer's Guide.*

Warning notices for posting up in appropriate premises include *cyanide poisoning*. More warnings today are issued in pocket card-form to be given to employees. Examples are *Wear Your Badge* (for radiation workers), *Asbestos Alert for the Construction Worker* and *Safe Working with Overhead Crane: Driver's Guide.*

Licences and certificates

Licences needed, for example, for the storage of petroleum are obtained from the local authority. A Certificate of Means of Escape in Case of Fire is needed by many – probably most – small firms. Application should be made to the fire authority or, in some cases, the fire brigade. A certificate indicating that a policy of insurance has been obtained covering employer's liability should be displayed.

For certain work, individual employees have to be trained and certified by you as employer as you appoint them to undertake such jobs as tool setting at power presses and mounting of abrasive wheels.

Records of statutory examination

Lifts, cranes, pressurised plant like steam boilers and air receivers have to be periodically examined by a competent person, usually an insurance company engineer or surveyor. All reports have to be kept on file.

It is compulsory to maintain all plant, machinery and equipment in a safe condition. Generally this means regular routine examination and maintenance for which adequate records should be kept.

Health records

For certain occupations where there is a special health risk, periodical medical examinations are required (e.g. for diving and certain work involving exposure to lead). Health registers have to be kept. Advice may be obtained from EMAS.

Notifications

Certain important matters have to be reported to the inspector such as:

- opening a new factory.
- reportable accidents.
- reportable dangerous occurrences.
- certain work with asbestos.
- certain diseases

New Regulations for the reporting of accidents, dangerous occurrences and diseases came into force on 1 April 1996, known for short as the RIDDOR Regulations. They tidy up the previous scattered law and extend its scope to some extent.

Accidents

The following events are notifiable where they occur in work-related circumstances.

- fatal accidents to employees, self-employed persons working on your premises or non-employees such as members of the public (e.g. customers)
- major injury accidents which occur to employees or self-employed persons
- major injury accidents to non-employees such as customers who are taken to hospital from your premises. (Major injuries include amputations for instance.)

You have to notify the local authority or the HSE, as the case may be, without delay (e.g. by telephone) and, within ten days, must submit a completed accident notice – Form 2508.

Also notifiable by sending in a Form 2508 are 'over three day' accidents. These are work-related accidents (including acts of violence) which cause an employee or a self-employed person working on your premises to be unable to do their normal work for over three days. This includes non-work days (e.g. weekends) generally.

Work-related diseases

Certain work-related diseases are notifiable on Form 2508A,

(e.g. dermatitis and occupational asthma). If a doctor informs you of an employee with such a disease, you have to notify the enforcing authority.

Dangerous occurrences

Certain dangerous occurrences, which could have caused a reportable injury, are also notifiable (e.g. when a tipping lorry or a crane contacts an overhead power line but no one is injured) so that it is not notifiable as an accident.

Firms which have to notify the local authority (environmental health officers) are those in the following categories:

- office-based
- retail or wholesale
- warehousing
- hotel and catering
- sports or leisure
- certain residential accommodation (but not nursing homes)
- those concerned with places of worship

A single copy of a short booklet, which outlines the main requirements and is called *Everyone's Guide to RIDDOR 95*, may be obtained free. Useful information is also included on the Form 2508, a copy of which is, incidentally, inside that booklet and which may be freely reproduced for notification purposes. If in doubt about any aspect of notification, contact the enforcing authority.

Posters and notices

As part of official policy to simplify legislation and reduce unnecessary burdens on business, a number of documents are no longer required to be posted up in workplaces. They have been carefully chosen so that important ones, like copies of Regulations, are still required. The documents which no longer need to be displayed include such fiddly ones as copies of Exemption Certificates, which few people read and even fewer understand. But, surprisingly, the forbidding notice of Health and Safety Law may be presented in a more user-friendly way – provided that the HSE expressly sanctions this.

20

your views

The Health and Safety Commission (HSC) has published a Discussion Document entitled 'Health and Safety in Small Firms' with the object of improving these matters in small firms. The HSC, together with the HSE, has the task of advising the government on law relating to health and safety at work (and elsewhere) while the HSE – and the local authorities – have the task of enforcement.

The document shows that the HSC is aware of some of the problems of small firms but is anxious to learn more. It accepts, for instance, that many employers find the laws difficult to understand, consider that there is too much paperwork and form filling, and many are wary in their approach to inspectors.

It is necessary to protect people from harm wherever they work and the laws governing safety at work should be easy to understand. The HSC would like to improve their relationship with small firms, remove unnecessary rules and paperwork, raise your awareness of the cost of accidents and work-related illnesses while giving priority for inspections at places where the risks are greatest.

The HSE seeks your views, so communicate with their nominated official:

> Joan Borley, Health and Safety Executive,
> Small Firms Unit, 7th Floor, North Wing,
> Rose Court, 2 Southwark Bridge,
> London SE1 9HS
> Fax: 0171 717 6417

The Discussion Document, if you choose to use it (and that is not necessary), contains some pages of questions for you to answer. Do not be afraid to speak your mind!

appendix 1: area office information services

Area offices

Members of the public who need advice on any aspect of the Health and Safety at Work Act 1974 should enquire at any of the 20 area offices listed below or at the HSE Information Centre. HSE area offices are open 9am to 5pm Monday to Friday.

Useful addresses

South West

Inter City House, Mitchell Lane, Victoria Street, Bristol BS1 6AN   Tel: 0117 988 6000   Fax: 0117 926 2998

Local authorities

Avon, Cornwall, Devon, Gloucestershire, Somerset, Isles of Scilly.

South

Priestley House, Priestley Road, Basingstoke RG24 9NW Tel: 01256 404000   Fax: 01256 404120

Local authorities

Berkshire, Dorset, Hampshire, Isle of Wight, Wiltshire.

South East

3 East Grinstead House, London Road, East Grinstead, West Sussex RH19 1RR Tel: 01342 334200   Fax: 01342 334222

Local authorities

Kent, Surrey, East Sussex, West Sussex.

London North

Maritime House, 1 Linton Road, Barking, Essex IG11 8HF Tel: 0181 235 8000   Fax: 0181 235 8001

Local authorities

Barking and Dagenham, Barnet, Brent, Camden, Ealing, Enfield, Hackney, Haringey, Harrow, Havering, Islington, Newham, Redbridge, Tower Hamlets, Waltham Forest.

London South

1 Long Lane, London SE1 4PG
Tel: 0171 556 2100   Fax: 0171 556 2200

Local authorities

Bexley, Bromley, City of London, Croydon, Greenwich, Hammersmith and Fulham, Hillingdon, Hounslow, Kensington and Chelsea, Kingston, Lambeth, Lewisham, Merton, Richmond, Southwark, Sutton, Wandsworth, Westminster.

East Anglia

39 Baddow Road, Chelmsford, Essex CM2 0HL
Tel: 01245 706200   Fax: 01245 706222

Local authorities

Essex except the London Borough of Essex covered by London N, Norfolk, Suffolk.

Northern Home Counties

14 Cardiff Road, Luton, Beds LU1 1PP
Tel: 01582 444200   Fax: 01582 444320

Local authorities

Bedfordshire, Buckinghamshire, Cambridgeshire, Hertfordshire.

East Midlands

Belgrave House, 1 Greyfriars, Northampton NN1 2BS
Tel: 01604 738300   Fax: 01604 738333

Local authorities

Leicestershire, Northamptonshire, Oxfordshire, Warwickshire.

West Midlands

McLaren Building, 35 Dale End, Birmingham B4 7NP
Tel: 0121 609 5200   Fax: 0121 609 5349

Local authorities

Birmingham, Coventry, Dudley, Sandwell, Solihull, Walsall,
Wolverhampton.

Wales

Brunel House, 2 Fitzalan Road, Cardiff CF2 1SH
Tel: 01222 263000   Fax: 01222 263120

Local authorities

Clwyd, Dyfed, Gwent, Gwynedd, Mid Glamorgan, Powys,
South Glamorgan, West Glamorgan.

Marches

The Marches House, Midway, Newcastle-under-Lyme,
Staffs ST5 1DT
Tel: 01782 602300   Fax: 01782 602400

Local authorities

Hereford and Worcester, Shropshire, Staffordshire.

North Midlands

The Pearsons Building, 55 Upper Parlaiment Street,
Nottingham NG1 6AU
Tel: 0115 971 2800   Fax: 0115 971 2802

Local authorities

Derbyshire, Lincolnshire, Nottinghamshire.

South Yorkshire and Humberside

Sovereign House, 110 Queen Street, Sheffield S1 2ES
Tel: 0114 291 2300   Fax: 0114 291 2379

Local authorities

Barnsley, Doncaster, Humberside, Rotherham, Sheffield.

West and North Yorkshire

8 St Pauls Street, Leeds LS1 2LE
Tel: 0113 283 4200   Fax: 0113 283 4296

Local authorities

Bradford, Calderdale, Kirklees, Leeds, Wakefield, Craven,
Hambleton, Harrogate, Richmondshire, Scarborough,
Selby, York.

Greater Manchester

Quay House, Quay Street, Manchester M3 3JB
Tel: 0161 952 8200   Fax: 0161 952 8222

Local authorities

Bolton, Bury, City of Manchester, City of Salford, Oldham,
Rochdale, Stockport, Tameside, Trafford, Wigan.

Merseyside

The Triad, Stanley Road, Bootle, Merseyside L20 3PG
Tel: 0151 479 2200   Fax: 0151 479 2201

Local authorities

Chester, Congleton, Crewe, Ellesmere Port, Halton,
Knowsley, Liverpool, Macclesfield, St Helens, Sefton, Vale
Royal, Warrington, Wirral.

North West

Victoria House, Ormskirk Road, Preston PR1 1HH
Tel: 01772 8362000   Fax: 01772 836222

Local authorities

Cumbria, Lancashire.

North East

Arden House, Regent Centre, Regent Farm Road,
Gosforth, Newcastle-upon-Tyne NE3 3JN
Tel: 0191 202 6200   Fax: 0191 202 6300

Local authorities

Cleveland, Durham, Newcastle-upon-Tyne,
Northumberland, North Tyneside, South Tyneside,
Sunderland.

Scotland East

Belford House, 59 Belford Road, Edinburgh EH4 3UE
Tel: 0131 247 2000   Fax: 0131 247 2121

Local authorities

Borders, Central, Fife, Grampian, Highland, Lothian,
Tayside, and the island areas of Orkney and Shetland

Scotland West

373 West George Street, Glasgow G2 4LW
Tel: 0141 275 3000   Fax: 0141 275 3100

Local authorities

Dumfries and Galloway, Strathclyde, and the Western Isles.

HSE

HSE Information Centre, Broad Lane, Sheffield S3 7HQ
Tel: 01142 892345
Fax: 01142 755792

HSE priced and some free publications are currently
available from:

HSE Books, PO Box 1999, Sudbury, Suffolk CO10 6FS.
Tel: 01787 881165

and from certain bookshops (priced publications).

HMSO

HMSO publications are sold through HMSO bookshops
and by mail order from:

HMSO Books, PO Box 276, London SW8 5DT. Tel: 0171
873 9090

HMSO bookshops

80 Chichester Street, Belfast BT1 4JY
258 Broad Street, Birmingham B1 2HE
Southey House, Wine Street, Bristol BS1 2BQ
71 Lothian Road, Edinburgh EH3 9AZ
49 High Holborn, London WC1V 6HB
9-21 Princess Street, Manchester M60 8AS

British Standards

British Standards are available from:

British Standards Institution, Sales Department, Linford
Wood, Milton Keynes MK16 6LE.
Tel: 01908 221166

Health

Employment Medical Advisory Service – see local telephone
directory.

appendix 2:
some key legislation

Statutes

Factories Act 1961
Fire Precautions Act 1971
Health and Safety at Work etc. Act 1974
Offices, Shops and Railway Premises Act 1963

Regulations

Asbestos Regulations 1969
Asbestos (Licensing) Regulations 1983
Construction (Design and Management) Regulations 1994
Construction (General Provisions) Regulations 1961
Construction (Working Places) Regulations 1966
Control of Asbestos at Work Regulations 1987
Control of Substances Hazardous to Health Regulations
    1988 ('COSHH')
Electricity at Work Regulations 1989
Health and Safety (Display Screen Equipment) Regulations
    1992
Management of Health and Safety at Work Regulations
    1992
Manual Handling Operations Regulations 1992
Personal Protective Equipment at Work Regulations 1992
Workplace (Health, Safety and Welfare) Regulations 1992

HSE area offices

HSE area offices (Open 9 am to 5 pm Monday to Friday)
Contact addresses and telephone numbers

Inter City House, Mitchell Lane, Victoria Street,
BRISTOL BS1 6AN
Tel: 0117 988 6000 (Fax: 0117 926 2998)
Covers – Avon, Cornwall, Devon, Gloucestershire,
Somerset, Isles of Scilly

Priestley House, Priestley Road,
BASINGSTOKE RG24 9NW
Tel: 01256 404000 (Fax: 01256 404 120)
Covers – Berkshire, Dorset, Hampshire, Isle of Wight,
Wiltshire

3 East Grinstead House, London Road,
EAST GRINSTEAD RH19 lRR
Tel: 01342 334200 (Fax: 01342 334222)
Covers – Kent, Surrey, East Sussex, West Sussex

Maritime House, 1 Linton Road, BARKING IGll 8HF
Tel: 0181 235 8000 (Fax: 0181 235 8001)
Covers – Barking and Dagenham, Barnet, Brent, Camden,
Ealing, Enfield, Hackney, Haringey, Harrow, Havering,
Islington, Newham, Redbridge, Tower Hamlets, Waltham
Forest

1 Long Lane, LONDON SEl 4PG
Tel: 0171 556 2100 (Fax: 0171 556 2200)
Covers – Bexley, Bromley, City of London, Croydon,
Greenwich, Hammersmith and Fulham, Hillingdon,
Hounslow, Kensington and Chelsea, Kingston, Lambeth,
Lewisham, Merton, Richmond, Southwark, Sutton,
Wandsworth, Westminster

39 Baddow Road, CHELMSFORD CM2 0HL
Tel: 01245 706200 (Fax: 01245 706222)
Covers – Essex (except the London Boroughs in Essex
covered by the Barking Office), Norfolk, Suffolk

14 Cardiff Road, LUTON LUl lPP
Tel: 01582 444200 (Fax: 01582 444320)
Covers – Bedfordshire, Buckinghamshire, Cambridgeshire,
Hertfordshire

Belgrave House, 1 Greyfriars, NORTHAMPTON NNl 2BS
Tel: 01604 738300 (Fax: 01604 738333)
Covers – Leicestershire, Northamptonshire, Oxfordshire,
Warwickshire

McLaren Building, 35 Dale End, BIRMINGHAM B4 7NP
Tel: 0121 609 5200 (Fax: 0121 609 5349)
Covers – Birmingham, Coventry, Dudley, Sandwell,
Solihull, Walsall, Wolverhampton

Brunel House, 2 Fitzalan Road, CARDIFF CF2 lSH
Tel: 01222 263000(Fax: 01222 263120)
Covers – Clwyd, Dyfed, Gwent, Gwynedd, Mid
Glamorgan, Powys, South Glamorgan, West Glamorgan

The Marches House, Midway,
NEWCASTLE-UNDER-LYME ST5 lDT
Tel: 01782 602300 (Fax: 01782 602400)
Covers – Hereford and Worcester, Shropshire, Staffordshire

The Pearsons Building, 55 Upper Parliament Street,
NOTTINGHAM NGl 6AU
Tel: 0115 971 2800 (Fax: 0115 971 2802)
Covers – Derbyshire, Lincolnshire, Nottinghamshire

Sovereign House, 110 Queen Street, SHEFFIELD S1 2ES
Tel: 0114 273 9081 (Fax: 0114 291 2379)
Covers – Barnsley, Doncaster, Humberside, Rotherham,
Sheffield

8 St Paul's Street, LEEDS LSl 2LE
Tel: 0113 283 4200 (Fax: 0113 283 4296)
Covers – Bradford, Calderdale, Kirklees, Leeds, Wakefield,
Craven, Hambleton, Harrogate, Richmondshire, Ryedale,
Scarborough, Selby, York

Quay House, Quay Street, MANCHESTER M3 3JB
Tel: 0161 952 8200 (Fax: 0161 952 8222)
Covers – Bolton, Bury, City of Manchester, City of Salford,
Oldham, Rochdale, Stockport, Tameside, Trafford, Wigan

The Triad, Stanley Road, BOOTLE, Merseyside L20 3PG
Tel: 0151 479 2200 (Fax: 0151 479 2201)
Covers – Chester, Congleton, Crewe, Ellesmere Port,
Halton, Knowsley, Liverpool, Macclesfield, St Helens,
Sefton, Vale Royal, Warrington, Wirral

Victoria House, Ormskirk Road, PRESTON PR1 1HH
Tel: 01772 836 200 (Fax: 01772 836 222)
Covers – Cumbria, Lancashire

Arden House, Regent Centre, Regent Farm Road,
Gosforth, NEWCASTLE UPON-TYNE NE3 3JN
Tel: 0191 202 6200 (Fax: 0191 202 6300)
Covers – Cleveland, Durham, Newcastle-upon-Tyne,
Northumberland, North Tyneside, South Tyneside,
Sunderland

Belford House, 59 Belford Road, EDINBURGH EH4 3UE
Tel: 0131 247 2000 (Fax: 0131 247 2121)
Covers – Borders, Central, Fife, Grampian, Highland,
Lothian, Tayside, Orkney and Shetland

375 West George Street, GLASGOW G2 4LW
Tel: 0141 275 3000 (Fax: 0141 275 3100)
Covers – Dumfries and Galloway, Strathclyde, and the
Western Isles

HSE Offshore Safety Division Offices

Lord Cullen House, Fraser Place, Aberdeen AB1 1UB
Tel: 01224 252500
Fax: 01224 252577

122A Thorpe Road, Norwich NR1 1RN
Tel: 01603 275000
Fax: 01603 275050

Merton House, Stanley Road, Bootle, Liverpool L20 3DL
Tel: 0151 951 4000
Fax: 0151 951 3158

index